I have known Jeff Voth for more than thirty years, and he epitomizes what it means to be a man of God. In this book he shares the secrets he has learned—through highs and lows of life—of how to be a man after God's own heart. *CaveTime* is full of passion, energy, humor, and wisdom. Every man needs to read this book and put it into practice.

—JAMES BRYAN SMITH, AUTHOR OF *THE APPRENTICE SERIES; ROOM OF MARVELS; A SPIRITUAL FORMATION WORKBOOK; EMBRACING THE LOVE OF GOD;* AND *RICH MULLINS: A DEVOTIONAL BIOGRAPHY: AN ARROW POINTING TO HEAVEN*

CaveTime is a book that focuses on the heart of male identity. What it means to relate to God, other men, and those in our lives that we love and cherish. *CaveTime* is about a calling. *CaveTime* is about values. *CaveTime* is about purpose. Jeff Voth cogently draws from his own journey and that of a multitude of men he has traveled with as a pastor, guide, and friend. *CaveTime* is biblical, timely, inspirational, and usably practical. Whether you are hungering for something more or a guide to other men, this book will be a valuable tool in navigating the complex tensions men face in the world today.

—HARVEY POWERS, PH.D. LICENSED CLINICAL PSYCHOLOGIST; LEADERSHIP COACH; FOUNDER OF THE REDIMERE GROUP: CENTER FOR COUNSELING AND LEADERSHIP DEVELOPMENT; BIBLE TEACHER; SEMINARY PROFESSOR

It has been my privilege to observe the lives of several men who have participated in Jeff Voth's *CaveTime*. The development of godly manhood has been the consistent result of their participation. Because "the proof of the pudding is in the eating," I heartily recommend *CaveTime*'s balanced approach to helping men grow into what God intended them to be.

—JIM GARRETT, AUTHOR OF *THE DOULOS PRINCIPLE*

I have seen and experienced firsthand the impact of a man spending time in the cave with his Creator and Savior. I watched my husband walk through a very dark period of his life with a deep desire to find freedom and understanding of who he was and is in Christ. Even after the darkness lifted, "going to the cave" became a daily habit and hunger for Jeff. And it still remains. This practice influenced our sons in a way that gave them a hunger to be men after God's heart by going to their own caves and becoming men of God. The effect this book has had and continues to have on myself and our daughter is life-changing, as we watch the men around us become a wall for those God places in their care. I would highly recommend this book not only to all men (no matter their age), but to women: wives, mothers, sisters, daughters. When men recognize their identity in Christ, women feel secure in their identity. The wall is built. Nurture is embraced, protection provided, and security experienced.

—LORI VOTH, WIFE OF JEFF THE CAVEMAN

Assaulted from every side, our men need a break. With a strong masculine voice, Jeff invites men to come along on the greatest adventure of their lives—encountering God in *CaveTime*. Wives, are you looking for a great gift for your stressed-out man? Buy him *CaveTime*, and he'll thank you!

—BECKY HARLING, SPEAKER,
AUTHOR OF *FREEDOM FROM PERFORMING*

CAVETIME

CAVETIME

GOD'S PLAN

FOR MAN'S

ESCAPE

FROM LIFE'S

ASSAULTS

JEFF VOTH

HONOR✛NET
PUBLISHERS

SAPULPA, OK

Published by HonorNet Publishers

P.O. Box 910
Sapulpa, OK 74067
Website: honornet.net

Dedication

Dedicated to Jesus, Lori, and King David

Contents

In the Cave

Overcome by the people and cares of his life,
David escaped to a place familiar to him.
A place of refuge.
A place he spent many nights as a young shepherd boy.
Now as a battle-worn warrior, carrying the weight of a
*   nation*
and only steps ahead of certain death, it would again be his
*   refuge.*
He knew this place.
He had dreamed here. Seen visions here.
Here in the cave, he had written songs and poems,
poured out his own heart, and heard God's voice.
His courage, strength, and boldness were born here, to kill
*   the lion, the bear, and Goliath.*

Only this time David would not be alone.
Other men came.
Those who were in distress, in debt, and discontented gath-
*   ered around him in the cave.*
Battle-proven warriors, now rejected and overcome with life,
*   they too were searching for a refuge.*
A place where they could once again find their honor,
*   strength, warrior status, and bare their souls without*
*   judgment.*

Something happened in the cave;
for they were later referred to as mighty men.

—JAKE JONES

Foreword

In *CaveTime,* Jeff Voth has done men a favor with this moving and creatively presented look at the story of David and his Mighty Men during their time in the cave, building themselves into an effective fighting force for their God. I have already begun to apply the principles he presents, including my personal favorite: "Just show up." Simply put, just like David and his warriors, regardless of who you are and what you've struggled with, report for duty and God can use you. How desperately the men in our culture need to hear that! I am truly thankful for Jeff, his message, and this book. Buy it, read it, soak it in.

—CLIFF GRAHAM, AUTHOR OF THE *LION OF WAR* BOOK SERIES,
INCLUDING *DAY OF WAR; COVENANT OF WAR; BENAIAH*

Acknowledgments

Lori: Thank you for covering me in my dark night. Without your prayers and your understanding, I might not have ever even made it out of the dark. I love you.

Jacob, Hannah, Caleb, and Cody: Thank you for giving me four reasons to be a wall.

Dad: Thank you for being my partner in fishing crime and for showing me grace and more grace. You stood as a wall and practiced the stones in front of us before we even knew what they were. We were safe because of you.

Jim Smith: Thank you for introducing me to the disciplines and for being an example of a grace-filled life. I'm blessed to have known you and I marvel at the good and beautiful things that God has done through you.

Jim Garrett: Thank you for being my sage. You have walked with me and been a wall of covering, grace, and truth.

Chad Craig: You were the first to make me think that this could be a book and that anyone would even want to read it. Thanks for pushing me to go to the lake, eat massive quantities of assorted meats, and put together the first crude manuscript (emphasis on crude).

Jake Jones: You get it. Thanks for showing up and making this happen.

Brad Lewis: You are an amazing editor. More importantly, you got inside of my head (sorry for your pain) and helped refine this book and make it a powerful tool in the lives of men.

Donny Howard: Thank you for being that crazy junior high kid in my youth group years ago, who has now grown into a mature (I use that term loosely) wall of a man for Emily and your kids. I am proud to be your pastor and to call you friend and cave brother. I'm also thankful that you stalked Cliff Graham on Facebook and set up that first meeting for us.

Brandon Walker: You were life to me in a dark time. You sought me out and joined me in the cave, as well as the duck blind, the goose blind, and that truck that was packed way too tight. You have become a wall for your girls and for Arvada High School, when no one else would.

Tom Farrell: You helped to make the book, the CD project, and the website come to life. Thank you for your consistency and the investments of your time, treasure, and talent.

Don Vance and Jeff Lamp: Your scholarly advice and insights have made this book academically stronger. Thank you for your involvement and for your friendship. I am honored to be your colleague.

David Osborn: Thank you for caring and for holding my feet to the fire during the project and thesis process. The pain was well worth the result.

Steve Cappa: You were a wing man like no other. Thanks for your encouragement, for sharing your expertise in men's issues with me, and for your unswerving commitment to this project. I am still jealous that you get to live in the Rockies.

As David had his Mighty Men, I too have had mine through the years. Their names are Jacob, Caleb, Cody, Kym, Tom, Money, Murph, Brad, Dave, John, Kenn, Helmsy, Jordan, Matt, Ferg, Moses, Jessee, Rick, Mark, Bobby, Jerry, Tim, Brandon, Maurice, Mike.

Nothing but fire kindles fire.

—Phillips Brooks

PREPARE FOR THE ASSAULT:
COME AND HIDE

M en are under assault.

Masculinity is under attack, blitzed by expectations and images that bombard us on every level. God expects something of us. Our families have their expectations of us. The culture certainly expects something of us. And we have our own expectations too. All of these expectations cause us to perform and strive, but for what?

At one point in my life, I couldn't answer the question "For what?" I felt like I was running and trying and doing and performing, but there was a hole in me. I knew this hole was unfilled and something needed to fill it. But the harder I tried to fill it myself, the more fatigued and exasperated I became.

I tried so hard that I ended up in panic and depression and eventually an emergency room.

The French philosopher Pascal said it best when he said: "This infinite abyss can be filled only with an infinite and immutable object; in other words, by God himself."

You've probably heard that before. I had a God-shaped hole I was trying to fill with works and people and material possessions. Nothing fit. In fact, when I tried to put anything else there, it hurt. I got to the point where I was so tired of trying and pushing and doing and straining that I actually wanted God to take me out. While I would not have killed myself, I would have been fine if He did.

I was done.

A Fatigued Heap of a Man

When I finally stopped, there God was—waiting for me, in the cave. That's the day I became a caveman. I'm not talking about some stupid Neanderthal who grunts and has no manners, or some patriarchal and condescending chauvinist who threatens to rule and reign. Instead, I became a tired, broken, worn-out, and fatigued heap of a man who didn't know who he was. The things that defined me had failed me and left me more confused than I'd ever been in my life.

Yet God was right there, whispering to me. "Come and hide," He gently said. "Come and escape and hide and be with Me. Only I can fill the hole...because I put it there."

Wow. God made me in His image, but He left a hole where only He could fit. Nothing else would ever fit in that space. And now here He was, in the cave, inviting me to come, and sit, and be filled.

I stumbled upon the narrative in 1 Samuel 17–25:16, which tells the story of King David of Israel and his fleeing, poverty-stricken, desperate group of friends. Like me, they had discovered the huge hole inside them. I thirsted for every word of this account—but it felt as if I was sipping it through a straw when I wanted to dump it like a bucket of water all over my life.

I read about David's meteoric rise to fame and then his equally swift and dizzying fall. Here was the famous teenager who had killed and beheaded the behemoth Goliath, but soon afterward found himself running for his own life. He quickly lost all that defined him and everything that brought him security and praise. He came to a place where he realized that he had nothing. He was nothing, and he was worth nothing. In fact, he was a liability. David had a God-shaped hole inside of him, and he was being chased by the insane King Saul who wanted to put a couple of holes on the outside of David as well!

David lost everything that defined him. All he knew to do was escape and hide…in the cave. "David departed from there and escaped to the cave" (1 Samuel 22:1, ESV).

Brothers of the Cave

Finally, in the quiet and darkness of a cave, David could show up and sit with his God, pray to his God, worship his God, and dwell on God's promises to him. Eventually, a group of men who needed to do the same things found David. These men would grow to love David so much that they would walk with him to hell and back if necessary. They became cavemen.

These brothers of the cave would now be defined and filled by God. After all, He had made them men in the first place. They would discover that God desired for each of them to be a representation of His masculine image on this planet. They would learn that only their Maker—the One whose image they bore—could fill, fulfill, define, and guide them through the incessant and repeated assaults leveled at them.

God was their only hope. And as He did with me, God whispered, "Come and hide. Come and escape and hide and be with Me. Only I can fill the hole…because I put it there." Their hope could only be found hiding with God in the dark.

Rocks and Roles

If the story ended there, this would be a very short book. But it doesn't! In the cave at Adullam, David and this group of 400 men went from fleeing and retreating escapees to becoming David and his Mighty Men.

Over time, these men became a group of celebrated warriors and protectors of their people. In the cave, they acquired skills to help them successfully deal with the forces that were chasing and trying to kill them on a daily basis. God also successfully equipped them to face future and inevitable assaults. In the cave, they developed some habits that I call "stones."

God wants the same for you as a man. In one of the Bible's most well-known stories, David slung a legendary stone at the giant Goliath (1 Samuel 17). As we move forward together through *CaveTime*, I will challenge you to get some stones. These are simple but powerful weapons you can use to kill the giants in your own life.

I will also challenge you to understand and begin to walk in what I see as three masculine roles that God has instilled in all men. I believe these roles are universal. They might look slightly or dramatically different from man to man, however, because each possessor of the X and Y chromosomes is a unique individual.

Because these roles are so foundational to what lies ahead, let's take a quick look at them:

Role 1: *Pursue an individual relationship with God first.* This role addresses what I call "first-ness." The first man, Adam, was created first. This doesn't mean I believe that men are better than women; this couldn't be further from the truth! Rather, being first speaks to a man's *role,* not his value.

Man indeed was created first for a purpose. God wants us as men to stand first. God created us to stand with Him first and to do that on a daily basis.

God also created Adam to think of his first gift, Eve, first. As we do the same in our lives, we will stand as a wall for those under our care. As a wall, we are to watch for attack. We'll stand in harm's way, if necessary, covering our mate and others we are responsible for.

In my opinion, as men, we were created to be God's primary instrument to help the people in our lives feel safe—physically, spiritually, and emotionally. If we can successfully do this over a period of time, then the people in our lives will gain the chance to accomplish what God has planned for them with less hesitation and less anxiety.

CaveTime will challenge you to be first with God and first on behalf of the people in your life, and it will equip you with the tools to do so.

Role 2: Understand that man was created to be a masculine presence on behalf of his God for the people in his world. As I've already stated, I believe that masculinity has been assaulted in our culture and men are confused. Because many of us have no idea what masculine even means, it's kind of tough to exercise a masculine presence. To be honest, we haven't had many role models who knew what masculinity meant. *CaveTime* will attempt to explain what it means to be masculine, as well as how we as men can hear from God on where and how to walk in that masculinity.

I also believe that men are called to represent God responsibly in the different arenas where we live our lives. This is where the *presence* aspect occurs. While the arenas where we live our lives as modern men might not be like the ones in ancient Rome—where the gladiators fought for their lives—our very real and present arenas can be found at home, school, work, and everywhere people in our culture live and move.

In these arenas of life, we exercise our masculine presence as real men and contend on behalf of those who look to us for physical, emotional, and spiritual sustenance and shelter. We also live out that presence among those who have no one to protect and cover them—those who are ignored and passed over by society. These individuals are in desperate need of a wall of men to protect them.

By the way, I believe these general roles are foundationally present in *all* men. Yet none of these roles will look exactly the same in *each* man. *CaveTime* will show you that just because a man has both X and Y chromosomes, he will not look exactly like the next guy does. Therefore, as you walk in your masculine presence, you will not look exactly the same as the men around you.

God wants unique men to take their masculine presence to the places where they live, in unique fashion, to build His Kingdom. I want you to know that God gives you permission to be unique, balanced, purposeful, and responsible on His behalf. This presence can come in many different packages. *CaveTime* will give you tools to operate as the unique man you are.

Role 3: Pursue relationships that help you to live well. By living
well, I mean living in healthy relationships that allow each party to be
built up and fully alive. As men, when we work for healthy relationships with our wives, we powerfully express the image of God to the
world. Our culture sees this relationship between a man and a woman
as a healthy community.

In Genesis 1:18, God created Eve, the first woman, as a "suitable
helper." This meant that Adam needed help. He could not do some
things without her. Adam simply could not see some perspectives
because he wasn't wired to. He needed a helper fit for him.

As a married man, the most complete way you can express the
entire personality of God is to have a thriving relationship with your
wife. To thrive, the two of you must spend time together physically,
emotionally, and spiritually. Again, *CaveTime* will challenge and equip
men to do just that.

A single man can also pursue healthy and appropriate relationships
with females. In these relationships, you build up one another, and
you don't cause the other to feel uncomfortable. These are relationships that focus on God's purpose in each other's lives, not purely the
pursuit of a relationship with a female. God's purpose, God's plan,
God's timing.

Of course, men also need healthy masculine relationships. We
need the accountability, camaraderie, and help of other men in our
struggle to live well and walk in our masculine roles. I believe that we
can find much power in healthy relationships with other men. These
relationships should build us up as men and help us live powerful,
adventurous, and wholesome lives—lives that enhance our masculine
presence, not detract from it.

It's no secret that men receive synergistic power from other men.
We can have relationships with other men that result in a force greater
than the energy of one guy alone. The force of these men's individual
lives, when combined, creates an energy that is almost immeasurable.
However, synergy can also work destructively. So the relationships we

pursue must be healthy. *CaveTime* will challenge you to find guys you can experience a healthy synergy with—a band of cave brothers, one like David and his Mighty Men had with each other.

I will challenge you to find a band of brothers and learn through *CaveTime* to be with them, at the right places, at the right times, and for the right reasons. You'll be challenged to have a lot of fun, but to have godly fun. I'll urge you to laugh with and at your brothers as well, but to laugh with and at the right things.

To be a band of brothers on a mission for God is powerful and exhilarating. To seek God together, with a band of brothers, is spiritually combustible and life-changing. To engage with the Word of the Living God as a band of brothers is the type of instruction that you can't get anywhere else. This type of interaction with a group of brothers isn't boring or religious. Instead, it can be transparent, empowering, accountable, and life-changing.

CaveTime will provide you with the instruction, the tools, and the daily challenge to gather a band of brothers and be gladiators, a wall of men, learning to be men together. What an adventure this life can be for a man, in healthy, fun, and adventurous masculine community with his band of brothers.

Prepared for the Assault

Yes, men are under assault, and masculinity is under attack. The assaults will come again. But the path of escape never changes. God continues to gently say, "Come and hide." For cavemen, the path to the cave is well-trodden and instinctive.

I know that you have been assaulted before. Perhaps even right now you find yourself in a daze because of the latest volley of shots aimed at you.

Gather yourself and let's escape the assaults and hide with God in the cave. As we hide there, I'll tell you my story of brokenness and grace, mistakes and more grace. This isn't some formula for perfection. Those never work. This is a plan of escape, hiding, repair, and direction. God's direction. His time. His filling.

CaveTime.

—Jeff Voth, Caveman

Mocked as I fell, broken man, with his bed in
* hell.*
Dug my own grave, I can hear all the voices say,
* "Hypocrite, O hypocrite." Lord please help.*
The end of my rope, I have no other place to go.
* Runaway, O runaway, Lord please help.*
Runaway, O runaway, Lord please help me.
Mercy, Lord have mercy on me.
Mercy, Lord have mercy on me.
Cry out to You, I cry out to You. Lord please
* help.*
Cry out to You, I cry out to You. Lord please
* help, me.*
Mercy, Lord have mercy on me.
Mercy, Lord have mercy on me.

"Escape" by David Gungor and John Arndt
From *CaveTime: The Escape, A Worship Experience*

We come to beginnings only at the end.

—William Throsby Bridges

Chapter 1

ESCAPE:
SCENES FROM DAVID'S LIFE

There I was, in the emergency room, flat on my back, hooked up to a heart monitor and numerous other medical devices.

As a pastor, I'd been here before, but never as the patient. I was the one giving encouraging words to the family. The one reading a psalm to the patient and praying for healing. The one who whispered under my breath as I walked to my car, "Poor guy, he looked pretty bad."

Now, I was *that* guy—the one who looked and felt pretty bad.

As the ER staff monitored me, I begin to wonder how I arrived at such a place in my life—a place where I might be having a heart attack. I thought I was in great physical health. In fact, I was on a ten-mile run when I started having pains in my left arm. I mustered enough strength to get home and have my wife, Lori, rush me to the hospital.

What was happening to me? That question and a million others raced through my mind as it spiraled out of control. I quickly discovered that I'd have plenty of time to answer my own questions; it was 10:00 p.m. and my doctor couldn't see me until the next day. So, the staff moved me to the cardiac unit where I bunked with guys who were—in my opinion—truly old enough to be having heart attacks! They looked to be in their 70s and 80s. They groaned and made the kinds of noises that old men who've had heart attacks usually make.

But I was only thirty-three years old.

After a long night of nurses taking my pulse and checking my heart rate twice as many times as they do on a regular hospital floor, morning came and so did my doctor. After checking my chart and doing the obligatory "Say ah" and "Breathe deep" while holding his stethoscope to my chest, he told me that he was ordering a treadmill test. He promised to return that afternoon to discuss the results.

The treadmill test certainly added to my confusion. I not only passed it with flying colors, but the people administering the test kept intensifying it and smirking when they couldn't get me to stop, pass out, or fall off the machine.

As I sat on the hospital bed waiting for my doctor—there with my octogenarian roommates who were still making old man noises—I was both nervous and confused. If I had serious heart problems, wouldn't my ticker explode on the treadmill with the workout I'd received? But I also knew what I felt the day before—that pain in my arm that radiated up into my chest.

Maybe I'm Crazy!

When my doctor came into the room, he had a look of concern, but nothing that indicated he was seriously worried and prepared to tell us to pull the family together and throw me a going away party. He smiled a bit as he told me that I'd impressed the staff by not passing out during my treadmill test. He said that neither they nor he felt anything was wrong with my heart. With that statement, I felt a strange mix of relief, embarrassment, and confusion.

Sure, I was relieved that my heart wasn't going to explode out of my chest in the foreseeable future. But I was a bit embarrassed because I was sure that my doctor thought that I was a faker. And yes, I was greatly confused because I felt like I had had a heart attack (at least a little one), and obviously I hadn't.

My doctor then asked me a series of questions that led down an even more unsettling path. He wanted to know what kind of stresses I was under, if I'd experienced any major emotional losses recently, what my vocation was, and if my family had any history of mental illness.

That last question stunned me! "He thinks I'm crazy," I said to myself. "Maybe I am," I answered back. "No you aren't," I retorted to myself. You know what they say if you start having a conversation with yourself, right? Maybe my physician was on to something.

Well, I must have answered the questions correctly enough to convince him that if I was crazy, I wasn't dangerous crazy. At least he didn't call the men in white suits and have them bring a straitjacket in my size.

He did explain, however, that my supposed heart attack the day before was very real, but also very much in my head. I'd experienced what he called a panic attack and was also showing signs of possible depression.

Then he said something that rocked my world: "I'd like for you to consider getting some counseling." Now I was pretty sure that he was the one who was insane.

You Must Mean Someone Else—or Do You?

This was absolutely impossible. I was the answer guy! I was the one who dispensed sage-like advice. I was a holy man—a man of the cloth. I encouraged people and helped them out of this sort of situation.

Maybe my doctor didn't know who he was talking to. He must have grabbed the wrong chart. I was Super Jeff and could handle everything (I might even ask for Jesus' help if I got in a pinch). I wasn't a nut job or a mental case. Counseling was for those kinds of people. What was he talking about?

As he allowed me a few minutes to deal with the bomb he'd dropped squarely in my lap, my physician helped me process what was going on in my life and inside my head. I quickly realized that in the last year I had experienced some major losses, including the sicknesses and deaths of several people very dear to me as a result of cancer and AIDS. I was also in the middle of some big financial decisions, didn't make quite enough money for us to get ahead, and had recently become a father for the fourth time with the birth of our son Cody.

In addition to all of these pressures, I was a junkie. I was addicted to performance—my drug of choice. I saw life as one big competition to achieve, win, be the best, live clean, and do well at all costs. Of course, in the right context, these thoughts can be fine. But I believed—wrongly, I might add—that in order to be loved, I had to perform at a certain level. I had to do so at home, at the church where I worked, and in my relationship with God.

I wouldn't have admitted to it before this emotional crash, but I really believed deep in my heart that for God to love me (and for that matter, for people to love me), I had to earn it. I spoke of grace, but I didn't accept it from God, and I didn't extend it all that well either. What's more I was the product of a culture that put pressure on a man to be a man, yet did nothing to help him find out what being one really meant.

I thought I had to be tough, suck it up, take the bull by the horns, kick butt, take on all comers, stand against the bad guys, and—for God's sake and in the name of all that is holy—never, never, ever cry or show weakness. That would mean I needed help. And real men, tough men, don't ever need help.

Under Attack

I felt attacked from every direction. I felt attacked by my doctor. I felt attacked by God. I felt attacked by my responsibilities. And I felt attacked by the fact that I wasn't measuring up as a man.

I also felt attacked by my mortality. How could my body fail me like that and act like it was having a heart attack? How dare my body do that!

I also felt attacked by my theology and my perception of who God was, because He sure wasn't coming through for me right now, and He sure hadn't come through for my loved ones who had died of cancer and AIDS.

There was also this gnawing in the pit of my stomach that wouldn't go away. I just felt sick.

Hopeless.

Have you ever felt this way? The truth is that all men in our culture are under some kind of assault. Enemies are all around. Attacks can come at any moment and from any direction. Defining the war and identifying our enemies are the first steps to mounting a counter-offensive, because we have to know who our battle is with.

One of the first enemies we must contend with is our basic image of what manhood really is. I believe that every man's understanding of masculinity has been distorted. This distortion began way back in the Garden of Eden, soon after the first man was placed upon this planet.

Because of this initial distortion, we have allowed the wrong people, forces, and voices to define who we are as men. The result is that we don't know who we are or how we're supposed to behave.

Consider one powerful voice speaking out loud about how men are portrayed in our contemporary culture, particularly in the ever-present voice of the media. Australian professor of public communication James Macnamara writes:

> Research reported in this paper shows that mass media are engaged in an active campaign of manufacturing contempt for men and traditional male identities in modern societies through representations that they portray.... Highly negative views of men and male identity provide little by way of positive role models for boys to find out what it means to be a man and gives boys little basis for self-esteem.... In the current environment where there is an identified lack of positive male role models in the physical world through absentee fathers in many families, and a shortage of male teachers, the lack of positive role models in the media and presence of overwhelmingly negative images should be of concern.... Ultimately such portrayals could lead to negative social and even financial costs for society in areas such as male health, rising suicide rates, and family disintegration. The idealized image of

the metrosexual (the softened and effeminate male)—largely a creation of the media—only further adds to the confusion being felt particularly by boys trying to find their identity in the modern world.[1]

Not only does the media actively assault men, our culture has a severe lack of male role models in families, schools, and the lives of many children. Confused boys and girls grow up to be confused men and women. Society is largely missing positive male images, perpetuating more and more confusion about masculinity with each passing generation.[2]

I'm not sure which assaults are more dangerous—the physical and immediate ones like David experienced or the cultural assaults just described. The attacks we face today from the media and our culture anesthetize slowly and subtly over a period of many years, shooting no real bullets and wielding no deadly spears or swords. But they seem just as dangerous as the very real, life-threatening assaults aimed directly at David.

An All-Out Attack

David experienced a 360-degree, all-out attack upon everything that he held near and dear. Everything that brought him security, value, and sustenance was taken from him. In seven scenes from David's life, we can see how the very real attacks he faced and the assaults we're under in the 21st century really aren't all that different.

Scene 1: Goliath dieth. David had often worshiped and played his harp for an audience of only God and his father's sheep on the hillsides of Bethlehem. He'd also been the victor in battles with wild beasts before. However, only God and the sheep could attest to this fact.

David recounted these exploits to Saul and a group of his commanders:

Your servant has been keeping his father's sheep. When a lion or a bear came and carried off a sheep from the flock, I went after it, struck it and rescued the sheep from its mouth. When it turned on me, I seized it by its hair, struck it and killed it. Your servant has killed both the lion and the bear (1 Samuel 17:34-36).

But now the entire nation was watching as David defended the honor of their God against that huge Philistine thug Goliath.

Maybe David should have been upset at the offensive taunts the behemoth was shouting at God. But a while back, David had been anointed king by the prophet Samuel. Something happened deep inside of him during the weird ceremony that consisted of prayer and anointing oil. Deep inside, David sensed a residing and palpable presence of God that caused him to feel an internal fire like nothing that he had ever experienced:

The LORD said to Samuel, "How long will you mourn for Saul, since I have rejected him as king over Israel? Fill your horn with oil and be on your way; I am sending you to Jesse of Bethlehem. I have chosen one of his sons to be king... You are to anoint for me the one I indicate"... "There is still the youngest," Jesse answered. "He is tending the sheep." Samuel said, "Send for him..." So he sent for him and had him brought in. He was glowing with health and had a fine appearance and handsome features. Then the LORD said, "Rise and anoint him; this is the one." So Samuel took the horn of oil and anointed him in the presence of his brothers, and from that day on the Spirit of the LORD came powerfully upon David (1 Samuel 16:1, 3, 11, 12-13).

Now, as he faced Goliath, David was feeling that power. He sensed the presence that brought the fire in his belly. What an epic battle—we pick it up right at the apex. All of the shouting and calling each other's mothers and relatives six generations back every name in the book was

over. God was with David, no doubt, and He was ready to silence the
giant. It was time to throw down in the name of the Living God:

> As the Philistine moved closer to attack him, David ran
> quickly toward the battle line to meet him. Reaching into
> his bag and taking out a stone, he slung it and struck the
> Philistine on the forehead. The stone sank into his forehead,
> and he fell face down on the ground. So David triumphed
> over the Philistine with a sling and a stone; without a sword in
> his hand he struck down the Philistine and killed him. David
> ran and stood over him. He took hold of the Philistine's sword
> and drew it from the sheath. After he killed him, he cut off
> his head with the sword (1 Samuel 17:48-51).

What can we learn from David in this situation? I think the lesson
is that God is calling men to stand for Him alone. Do you remember
Role 1? God created individual men to have an individual relationship
with Him and stand with Him alone.

Not one other man dared to stand against Goliath that day. All the
others were petrified. When you look at the situation David walked
into, you'll see that the men on the battlefield needed someone to be
a man and step up. It would definitely have to be a man stepping up
alone, because "all" of the men fled, even their king:

> Early in the morning David left the flock in the care of a shep-
> herd, loaded up and set out, as Jesse had directed. He reached
> the camp as the army was going out to its battle positions,
> shouting the war cry. Israel and the Philistines were drawing
> up their lines facing each other. David left his things with
> the keeper of supplies, ran to the battle lines and asked his
> brothers how they were. As he was talking with them, Goliath,
> the Philistine champion from Gath, stepped out from his lines
> and shouted his usual defiance, and David heard it. Whenever
> the Israelites saw the man, they all fled from him in great fear
> (1 Samuel 17:20-24).

David, however, was willing to stand alone, with thousands watching. He'd stood alone many times before, when his only audience was God and the sheep he was tending. Because of that individual relationship, forged in his solo time with God, David knew that he was a man (albeit a very young one). He was ready to step up and exercise his masculine presence on behalf of the Lord that he knew so well and loved so much. He couldn't just sit and allow the forces of evil to deride and curse Him. He was willing to be a man and stand for those who would not and could not do it for themselves. As he operated in Role 1 (standing alone with God), David was enabled to take on Role 2 (being a masculine presence on behalf of God).

After standing alone and establishing his masculine presence, David stepped into an authority that allowed him to rally the army of the Lord to victory and bring together the men in a powerful community that struck fear into the enemy. You see where I'm going, don't you? David's actions enabled Role 3 to take place. Watch it happen.

> Then the men of Israel and Judah surged forward with a shout and pursued the Philistines to the entrance of Gath and to the gates of Ekron. Their dead were strewn along the Shaaraim road to Gath and Ekron (1 Samuel 17:52).

Because David knew how to stand alone with God (Role 1), he knew that God was there with him, directing him when and where and how to stand and establish and walk in his masculine presence (Role 2). Because David assumed these roles, men rallied around him and to him. This created a magnetism that God sent to the men on that battlefield, unleashing the positive synergistic effect of Role 3. David drew these men together to live well.

The same thing can happen to us today as we stand with our God alone and are willing to walk in our masculine presence. I believe that God brings to us other men who want the same thing. He has a band of brothers marked for us to gather into a community of Philistine-chasing madmen. God wants His men to form a group to rally and fight the battles of the Kingdom—to fight for our wives and our sons and our daughters. These men are looking for someone to stand and invite them to get together and spend some time with God. Maybe they need one man with a fire in his gut to step up and be the first to volunteer. Maybe they need someone to step up and be the point man who they will follow.

Men standing, taking their presence into their world together. This initiates a process that strikes fear into the enemy and fire into the hearts of men.

When David took out Goliath, a fearful community of hiding men turned into a powerful community of Philistine-chasing warriors. This band of brothers could now chase their enemies all the way to Goliath's front porch.

These men possessed the same X and Y chromosomes they had before. But now one man was willing to stand and gather them. And in order to make sure that everyone knew it was safe to step into their masculine presence, David showed them that at least one giant would not be intimidating anyone anymore:

> David took the Philistine's head and brought it to Jerusalem;
> he put the Philistine's weapons in his own tent (1 Samuel 17:54).

I know this is totally barbaric, but every time I read about David parading around with Goliath's head, I want to paint my face like William Wallace in *Braveheart* and go pick a fight! (Of course, I know real godly men don't just "pick a fight.") David wanted the men of the army and their leaders and the people who lived in God's city to know that they had no need to live in fear. Their God, working through men who would stand for Him, had begun to raise up men who would be a wall of protection.

David made quite a statement that day as he walked powerfully in all three masculine roles. I certainly can't blame him for holding on to that huge Philistine cranium for a trophy. I'm pretty sure he didn't just haul it back to Jerusalem to throw it away. I believe he got it stuffed and put it on the mantel above his fireplace.

Scene 2: Falling rock star. After the amazing encounter in Scene 1, I'm sure David thought that he was set for a great and successful life. Who could blame him? God was surely with him. And King Saul had promised some pretty nice prizes for the one who killed Goliath, so David would surely be living on Easy Street for the rest of his days:

> Now the Israelites had been saying, "Do you see how this man keeps coming out? He comes out to defy Israel. The king will give great wealth to the man who kills him. He will also give him his daughter in marriage and will exempt his family from taxes in Israel" (1 Samuel 17:25).

David could also expect some type of high-level job offer to work in the king's security detail. After all, who wouldn't want a giant killer as a personal body guard? For a while, things were perfect for David and his bride—the king's daughter, Michal—as they settled into their new home and enjoyed David's newfound fame. David was such a rock star that songs and poems were written about him:

> When the men were returning home after David had killed the Philistine, the women came out from all the towns of Israel to meet King Saul with singing and dancing, with joyful songs and with timbrels and lyres. As they danced, they sang: "Saul has slain his thousands, and David his tens of thousands" (1 Samuel 18:6-7).

Unfortunately, Camelot isn't located just north of Jerusalem and things quickly fell apart. David did his best to operate in his three masculine roles. He was trying to live right, love his wife, do his job well, serve his employer faithfully, all for the glory of God.

However, the initial sign that the fabric of life was coming apart at the seams actually happened one night while David conducted a house concert at his father-in-law's place. David's music seemed to soothe

the effects of the demonically induced migraines that vexed the old monarch. Yes, Saul loved to hear anointed songs with the accompaniment of harp and lyre.

However, as David was in the middle of a killer lyre solo, he almost got himself killed:

> [Saul] was prophesying in his house, while David was playing the lyre, as he usually did. Saul had a spear in his hand and he hurled it, saying to himself, "I'll pin David to the wall." But David eluded him twice. Saul was afraid of David, because the LORD was with David but had departed from Saul. So he sent David away from him and gave him command over a thousand men, and David led the troops in their campaigns. In everything he did he had great success, because the LORD was with him. When Saul saw how successful he was, he was afraid of him (1 Samuel 18:10-15).

What a sucker punch this must have been for David. He probably didn't see it coming—at least the first time. If this wasn't a message to David that something was wrong—at least in the eyes of Saul—I don't know what it was. However, as abusers often do, Saul showered David (the abused) with a gift, giving him the command of a thousand men. I'm sure that David tried to rationalize the incident away and make it less than it was: attempted murder.

We all do this, though, so we can't really blame David. Plus, abusers can be very charming. However, as abusers always do, unless they get help, they abuse again and again.

> While David was playing the lyre, Saul tried to pin him to the wall with his spear, but David eluded him as Saul drove the spear into the wall. That night David made good his escape (1 Samuel 19:9-10).

David could now be sure his position had been terminated! Instead of a pink slip, Saul tried to make David into a kabob. David realized that he'd minimized the last incident. The rock star had officially been fired.

I think it's worth noting Saul's motive for the attempted and repeated skewerings of his son-in-law. The revelation is found in both 1 Samuel 19:12 and 15. Do you see it? Both verses state that Saul was "afraid" of David.

Afraid? Wow! Saul's actions seem more like aggression to me. Anger, fury, spear flinging, and tempestuous rage seem a bit more accurate.

Saul feared David. He was fearful that David was going to take his kingdom away, so Saul had to do what in his demon-crazed mind made sense. Fear manifests itself in many different ways, shapes, and forms. But we can safely say that anyone experiencing fear wants the cause of the fear to be out of the picture. So Saul chucked a spear at his fear.

Way back in the Garden of Eden, the enemy was afraid of God and afraid of God manifesting Himself in a man, Adam. The enemy was also afraid of God manifesting Himself in David. And the enemy is still afraid that God will manifest Himself in you too.

Satan also would have been fine if I'd had a real heart attack or just stayed in my panic-stricken, anxiety-riddled, locked-up, and depressed place there in the ER. But there was hope for David, there was hope for me, and there is hope for every one of us today as well. It's right there in 1 Samuel 19:14. Do you see it? It's the word "with." God was *with* David. When God is *with* a man, the enemy is afraid of him.

When God is *with* you, you are a serious threat to the enemy and his forces. So he will do whatever he can to take you out.

What lesson can we learn from seeing David, the fallen rock star? One lesson is that life will not always go smoothly as you live out your roles. But even when life is tough, it doesn't necessarily mean you are doing anything wrong. In fact, you may be doing everything just right! You just happen to be in the middle of a battle—an all-out assault— and God wants you to know that He is with you.

I can guarantee you that as a man of God, the going *will* get rough. Camelot will come under assault. And the enemy of your soul will do his very best to hit you in the face with a spear or two. But none of that means that God is not still *with* you. He is still right there and you are still *the man*.

The only difference is that you are the man under assault.

You might be wondering how I can say with such confidence that you are still the man and that you can be assured that God will still be with you. Notice that never once in this narrative does it say that the Lord ever left David and was not with him. David was scared. David was anxious. David was fearful of his life being taken. And yes, David even does some stupid and sinful things. But never once do we read that David was alone and that God was not with him.

Good thing, because David was about to be assaulted again…but God would still be with him.

Scene 3: Assault at Camelot. While at home, David learned from his wife that Saul (her father and his former employer) had sent a hit squad to their house to kill David:

> Saul sent men to David's house to watch it and to kill him in the morning. But Michal, David's wife, warned him, "If you don't run for your life tonight, tomorrow you'll be killed." So Michal let David down through a window, and he fled and escaped. Then Michal took an idol and laid it on the bed, covering it with a garment and putting some goats' hair at the head. When Saul sent the men to capture David, Michal said, "He is ill." Then Saul sent the men back to see David and told them, "Bring him up to me in his bed so that I may kill him." But when the men entered, there was the idol in the bed, and at the head was some goats' hair. Saul said to Michal, "Why did you deceive me like this and send my enemy away so that he escaped?" Michal told him, "He said to me, 'Let me get away. Why should I kill you?'" (1 Samuel 19:11-17).

David had lost his job. And now he was losing his marriage. Yes Michal informed David of the plot on his life. But she decided not to go with her man when he ran for it. I think she was hedging her bets and staying with Daddy, because she probably figured that David would be caught and killed anyway. To solidify her position, Michal also lied and claimed that David had threatened to kill her. I'm sure that this didn't help Daddy get over his David issues.

What lesson can we learn from this assault? The enemy hates the power of a man and a woman together, because a strong marriage represents the image of God to the world. Satan would do anything and everything to assault a marriage.

Just as David's marriage was a target, if you are married, your relationship has a huge bull's-eye on it. For that matter, every marriage is a target and will be assaulted again and again.

David went from being a rock star giant killer to being separated from his wife. He used to have it all together, but now almost nothing was for sure in his life anymore. However, David could be absolutely certain of two things: the enemy was not done assaulting him yet, and God was still with him (even if David didn't feel like He was).

Scene 4: Assaulted sage. After David narrowly escaped the assassination attempt at his own home and was separated from his wife, he fled to be with Samuel. This old holy man had been David's spiritual guide, mentor, and sage for many years. David probably felt that he could receive some type of spiritual consolation and have the prophet's comforting presence. And surely Saul wouldn't try to kill an innocent man in Samuel's presence.

However, demonic beings and the kings who play host to them don't care who is around. So when word got to Saul from a certain snitch that David was staying with the old prophet at Samuel's place, our fallen star fell once more:

When David had fled and made his escape, he went to Samuel at Ramah and told him all that Saul had done to him. Then he and Samuel went to Naioth and stayed there. Word came to Saul: "David is in Naioth at Ramah"; so he sent men to capture him (1 Samuel 19:18-20).

What lesson can we learn from this assault? The devil will pursue a man he fears anywhere and everywhere. The astonishing thing about this scene is how the fear driving Saul was so strong that he didn't hesitate to face off with the old prophet Samuel, in spite of his respect for him. The enemy in Saul feared David and his relationship with Samuel so much that he wanted to take that from him as well. David had also seen Saul's rage against him and his own son Jonathan, so what would keep him from killing the prophet? Probably nothing.

The enemy fears the relationships you will have with sages and mentors in your life, and he will try and keep you from engaging in them. Satan doesn't want you to be taught and schooled in the things of God. I've wondered what would have happened if David had decided to take his chances while staying with Samuel and fight it out. But we'll never know, because David was out of there before a fight could break out. And God was still with him.

Scene 5: Assaulted brotherhood. Next David escaped to his best friend's house. This was Jonathan, who was Saul's son. Together, David and Jonathan cooked up a plan to see whether or not it might be safe for David to come to dinner again. Maybe it could all be better again. Maybe Samuel had gotten through to Saul and rid him of his demons. Maybe this was all a bad dream:

> Then Jonathan said to David, "I swear by the LORD, the God of Israel, that I will surely sound out my father by this time the day after tomorrow! If he is favorably disposed toward you, will I not send you word and let you know? But if my father intends to harm you, may the LORD deal with Jonathan, be it ever so severely, if I do not let you know and send you away in peace" (1 Samuel 20:12-13).

Unfortunately, Saul, a vexed and paranoid monarch, was still as insanely angry and jealous as ever. He even lashed out violently at his own son in accusatory fashion. As Jonathan angrily stormed away from the dinner table, he signaled to David that his life was still in danger and that he should run for the hills:

> Jonathan got up from the table in fierce anger; on that second day of the feast he did not eat, because he was grieved at his father's shameful treatment of David....Jonathan said to David, "Go in peace, for we have sworn friendship with each other in the name of the LORD, saying, 'The LORD is witness between you and me, and between your descendants and my descendants forever.'" Then David left, and Jonathan went back to the town (1 Samuel 20:34, 42).

Our rock star was falling again as his relationship with his best friend was under assault as well. He officially had no one left to help him and offer security.

What can we learn from this assault? One of the most powerful lessons I see here is that the enemy fears healthy and deep relationships between bands of brothers who are intent on serving God together. Jonathan and David wanted God's purposes to be done through them and their family, and they were willing to risk their lives for it. They were living out Role 3, the pursuit of relationships that helped them to live well. They understood healthy masculine community. They were committed to helping each other live and live well. They were willing to lay down their lives for each other and elevate the other to the status of king.

In fact, Jonathan showed the depth of his commitment to God's will in their lives by giving David his robe and his weapons. As the king's son, the throne would have been Jonathan's. However, I'm sure Jonathan had heard of the ceremony that occurred years ago as Samuel had anointed David as future king.

Men who will be walls individually are powerful, but when the synergy of two or three brothers is in effect, kingdoms can be set in motion. That's exactly what happened between these brothers. The community found between these two men helped to usher in God's plan.

The words describing the commitment between David and Jonathan speak of a depth of brotherhood that most men never experience. What's more, the devil fears and fights this kind of relationship with all his might. The devil hates men operating in Role 3 and fears these types of masculine relationships that Scripture describes as being "one in spirit." What an amazing kinship.

> Jonathan became *one in spirit* with David, and he loved him as himself. From that day Saul kept David with him and did not let him return home to his family. And Jonathan made a covenant with David because he loved him as himself. Jonathan took off the robe he was wearing and gave it to David, along with his tunic, and even his sword, his bow and his belt (1 Samuel 18:1-4, emphasis added).

Their oneness is described later in the text in these terms:

> So Jonathan made a covenant with the house of David, saying, "May the LORD call David's enemies to account." And Jonathan had David reaffirm his oath out of love for him, because *he loved him as he loved himself* (1 Samuel 20:16-17, emphasis added).

The reason the enemy fears this "oneness" is due to the fact that God is one. The Godhead is made up of God the Father, God the Son, and God the Holy Spirit. When men emulate that relationship by being one in spirit, they are unstoppable. They become like the Spartan Phalanx and are impenetrable, moving and striking as one unit.

The day David left turned out to be the last time he'd see Jonathan this side of heaven. Several years later, upon hearing of Jonathan's death, the rock star wrote and sang one of the saddest laments on record. The last line describes the power of Role 3 and the depths that healthy masculine community can reach.

> I grieve for you, Jonathan my brother; you were very dear to me. Your love for me was wonderful, more wonderful than that of women (2 Samuel 1:26).

When David left his kindred spirit Jonathan in the field that day, he was truly alone and devoid of all human security, friendship, and help. But again, God was still with him.

Scene 6: Assault against common sense. After saying goodbye to Jonathan, David headed for the hills. But he realized that in his haste, he had not taken any supplies to sustain him. And he had no clue how long that might be. So he stopped at a church, found a priest, and ignored all religious polity by taking holy bread. Then he lied about his reasons:

> David answered Ahimelek the priest, "The king sent me on a mission and said to me, 'No one is to know anything about the mission I am sending you on.' As for my men, I have told them to meet me at a certain place. Now then, what do you have on hand? Give me five loaves of bread, or whatever you can find." But the priest answered David, "I don't have any ordinary bread on hand; however, there is some consecrated bread here—provided the men have kept themselves from women" (1 Samuel 21:2-4).

As David gathered the bread for his kosher sandwiches, he thought of another pretty big mistake he'd made: he had no weapon. So he pressed the priest for one, and David learned that the only thing available for killing was the huge sword that he had taken from Goliath in that epic confrontation on the battlefield between the armies of the Lord and the Philistines years earlier. I'm sure David reminisced about that glorious day for a split second, maybe a smile almost coming across his panic-stricken brow as he thought, "I picked a fight with that pagan scum on that day and I was *the man!"* David quickly returned to reality and nodded as he said that he would take the sword.

> The priest replied, "The sword of Goliath the Philistine, whom you killed in the Valley of Elah, is here; it is wrapped in a cloth behind the ephod. If you want it, take it; there is no sword here but that one." David said, "There is none like it; give it to me" (1 Samuel 21:9).

When the priest went to retrieve the sword, he had to haul out the monstrosity on a two-wheeled dolly. This was one huge piece of cutlery! David got behind the cart, mustered his energy to push, and then continued his trek toward the hills. He knew that it would be difficult for a redhead pushing a gigantic sword on a two-wheeled cart to hide very easily.

David's concerns proved to be true, because a murderous snitch waited nearby and was sure to tell Saul:

> Now one of Saul's servants was there that day, detained before the LORD; he was Doeg the Edomite, Saul's chief shepherd (1 Samuel 21:7).

What lesson can we learn from this assault? Run from anyone named Doeg? Perhaps, but the one that comes to my mind first is that when you are running for your life and in a panicked state, you often forget the most obvious of provisions and lose your common sense.

Have you ever done this? I have.

Many men are running today, living life in a panicked state and at a frenzied pace, forgetting that they have weapons at their disposal. They have God, who will hide them and meet with them in the cave. God will speak to them through His Word and prayer. God will give them a band of brothers to fight on His behalf.

Even though David was the most skilled of warriors, he didn't even remember the most basic commonsense provisions. He forgot food and his weapons. How scared and frazzled he must have been.

The enemy loves to make a man run and react to the assaults being waged upon his life. When that occurs, we forget the most basic things. Just like David forgot his sword and his food in his panicked state, men often forget their weapons and basic provisions for spiritual survival.

I don't know about you, but I don't often forget to stop and eat. In fact, I plan many of my days by taking into consideration where I am going to eat! Just as I put a lot of thought into where and how I will feed my body each day, I need to make arrangements to feed myself on the Word of God.

Having CaveTime will give me the weapons to do this each day (we'll get to these later when we look at five spiritual stones God provides to knock down the giants we face in our lives).

I must also learn to protect myself by taking up the sword of God's Word. While I need to learn how to use the Word of God for spiritual sustenance, I must also remember to use it to defend myself against the enemy. When I live a frazzled and panicked life, I often forget to take these provisions with me. But when I spend time in the cave learning to use these weapons, I'll remember to use the common sense God gave me to feed myself and to fight.

David did neither of these. His common sense was totally gone. He was running, his life was being threatened, he was panicked and making stupid mistakes. And yet, God was still with him.

Scene 7: Assaulted face. On his way to the mountains, in the middle of his panic and distress, David concocted a plan that seemed good to him. However, make a note to yourself that making plans that your life depends on during a time of extreme panic often doesn't work out so well.

David's plan was to go to Gath. Does that name sound familiar? Gath happened to be the hometown of the late giant Goliath and his four very large brothers.

What was David going to do in Gath? Seek refuge? That would be kind of an odd approach given that he'd viciously dismembered one of their most celebrated heroes. Or maybe David planned to muster up some of his old glory by beating up one of Goliath's brothers. The narrative doesn't tell us exactly why David went to Gath, but it was definitely an unconventional maneuver. The plan turned out about as good as you would have expected it to—not very:

> That day David fled from Saul and went to Achish king of Gath. But the servants of Achish said to him, "Isn't this David, the king of the land? Isn't he the one they sing about in their dances: 'Saul has slain his thousands, and David his tens of thousands'?" (1 Samuel 21:10-11).

David didn't seem to be revered or feared at all by his old enemies anymore. Achish's servants were mocking David, singing one of his old songs to him. Remember when the people were singing and dancing back in 1 Samuel 18:6-7? This was the song that propelled David to rock star status. But now the great and ferocious rock star warrior was being mocked with his own theme song. Ouch.

This scene reminds me of the time my boys and I happened to see the band KISS, famous in the 1970s and 1980s, as they sang during the TV halftime show of a Super Bowl. I'll admit that the visual of some old rock stars in spandex—way past their prime, but trying to sing their old songs—is painfully humorous. But as I watched my sons respond to this shocking and embarrassing spectacle, I was just flat amused.

They only kind of knew who KISS was, but instinctively they knew that something was just plain wrong with what they were watching. Their mouths fell wide open and they said almost in unison, "Who is that? What are they wearing? Why are they wearing it? Is that singing supposed to sound good? Are they the ones who are famous for that song?"

When my sons tried to look away, they responded like many people do when driving by a traffic accident—they wanted to look away but weren't able to. Once they got through the traffic accident stage, my boys started to sing and flail around and just mock KISS. I had to laugh too, but more at them than the old guys in spandex. It was just hilarious.

There was a day when people would pay huge money for KISS tickets and do almost anything to get into a concert. But that was long ago. And to my boys, KISS was now a laughingstock.

Apparently, that's what the guards at the gate thought about David. Laughing, flailing, and mocking. How utterly embarrassing. How startling and degrading it must have been for David to endure. It was a bad idea for David to come to Gath. They not only didn't fear him any longer, they were mocking him.

Coming to Gath was also a bad idea because instead of intimidating Achish, the king, David's presence just agitated him.

> Achish said to his servants, "Look at the man! He is insane! Why bring him to me? Am I so short of madmen that you have to bring this fellow here to carry on like this in front of me? Must this man come into my house?"(1 Samuel 21:14-15).

David quickly realized that he was no longer feared by these people and that the king was upset he was there at all. I also think that David realized that not only was he in danger of being beheaded by Saul's death squad, but also that Goliath's relatives wanted to systematically dismember him and feed him to the "birds of the air and the beasts of the earth"—the very thing David had threatened and then did to their champion Goliath.

> David took these words to heart and was very much afraid of Achish king of Gath. So he pretended to be insane in their presence; and while he was in their hands he acted like a madman, making marks on the doors of the gate and letting saliva run down his beard (1 Samuel 21:12-13).

David's survival instinct kicked in and he acted crazy—spitting on himself, licking the dirt, and chewing on a gatepost or two. Maybe he even used the bathroom on himself for good measure.

The king of Gath, being superstitious—as most monarchs of his day were—thought that if you killed a crazy person, his insanity could in fact come upon you. Therefore, he wanted nothing to do with David. How embarrassing! Once a rock star, and now he wasn't even worth killing. He must have felt that he wasn't valuable either in life or in death.

What an utter failure David had become. And yet, God was with him.

It Doesn't Fit Anymore

Can you relate? Imagine David acting like a fool and spitting on himself, posing and looking like an idiot. Have you ever acted like a fool? Looked like an idiot? Have you posed? Have you tried to muster some old glory to make yourself feel good? I'm embarrassed to say that I've been there, done that.

One day I was up in our attic looking for something. During my search I noticed a box with my mom's writing that said "Jeff's memories." I opened the box, and I swear I heard a heavenly choir in hallowed tones singing the Arvada High School's fight song. Then for the first time in twenty-five years, I saw a beloved relic. Brace yourselves: my old wrestling singlet.

As I picked up this smelly, musty, and once sweat-laden old friend, my mind began to travel. I went back in time to 1979, and I could hear the crowds chanting my name as I prepared to take the mat against my opponent. I could picture the cheerleaders, my parents, my friends, the opposing team, and the guy I was about to wrestle. What great days those were. And everything was fine on my trip down memory lane until I made one fatal mistake.

I decided to try on that old singlet.

No one was up in the attic, so what harm could be done? Maybe I should put it on and stand there in my old wrestling stance. I could recapture the feeling of having on my wrestling gear. Plus it would make my trip down memory lane more realistic.

So I stripped down and tried to pull on my old dusty friend, only to find that it wasn't so friendly anymore.

If you don't know what a wrestling singlet is, it is little more than underwear with some shoulder straps. My singlet looked a lot smaller than I remembered it. Of course, I failed to consider that I was fifty pounds heavier and my body had, shall we say, settled a bit.

I pushed forward with my plan, but I was only able to get the archaeological relic up to my mid-shins. I bent down and tried to pull the straps over my shoulders. I got the straps in place, but I couldn't stand upright or really move at all.

This thing was tight! I must have looked like ten pounds of sausage stuffed into a five-pound tube. If I didn't free myself pretty soon, I might pass out, tear a tendon, or blow out a knee and no one would ever find me up in the attic.

I must have looked absolutely ridiculous trying to feel young again. What did my little trip down memory lane get me? Well, it motivated me to go on a diet and to never try on that singlet again.

Maybe you haven't tried to fit into your old singlet, but many of us try to vicariously relive the fantasies of our past glory days and get fulfillment somewhere other than through a deep and powerful relationship with our Creator. Many men take on newfound competitive endeavors. Others try to engage in what they think is harmless flirting with other women at the office, the restaurant, or on the Internet. In some skewed way, we think these pursuits will help us feel like we did when we were young. While they might do that for a short period of time, like a shot of adrenaline, they are little more than distractions in our lives from being the men that God wants us to be.

These distractions can also end up being embarrassing, much like me in the attic trying to fit into my ancient wrestling singlet, or David trying to beat up on some old rivals in Gath with Goliath's sword. Taking matters into our own hands in the midst of the assaults being waged upon us usually doesn't work out so well.

In an effort to feel young again, David showed his face in a dangerous place and got himself in big trouble. After people recognized him as the former heroic warrior of Israel, David was arrested and taken before the king of Gath. He was in danger of being tried and executed on the spot. There were no public defenders around to take his case.

A meteoric rise to fame through the miraculous slaying of a giant by a God-ordained rock and slingshot, and now David was being ridiculed in the behemoth's hometown as a lunatic. He might even lose his life. What odd irony that would be. From cultural icon and hero to ridiculed outlaw.

David was being assaulted on every front, seeing every one of his support systems attacked and eventually obliterated. Wait a minute! Wasn't he supposed to be the king of Israel? He didn't even know anymore. Maybe it didn't really happen.

What had David done to deserve all of this? All he did was try and serve God and represent Him well. He had just tried to do his job, which was to play heavenly music for Saul, and Saul tried to kill him, repeatedly. And yet God was with him.

Where had David's courage gone? Where was the studly redheaded kid who was scared of absolutely nothing? Where were all of the cheers and songs that filled the air just a short time ago? Now the air was filled with spears and jeers, insults and unanswerable questions. All David really knew was that he was confused, in trouble, and had no support systems left. No job, no wife, no best friend, no mentor, and certainly no dignity. And yet God was with him.

David was down to just two options. One option was to kill himself. However, as much of a failure as he'd been up to this point, he would mess up that as well. So he had to take the second option: escape.

He knew he had to escape to a place where he could hide, get out of the bull's-eye, and chase after some direction from the One he faintly remembered calling him to be king in the first place.

Yes, he would go, hide, and listen for that voice. He knew he needed to clear his head and hopefully keep it connected to his torso.

With spit on his face and dirt on his teeth, he would escape. And God was still with him.

Through the darkness, through the fire, through
   my wicked heart's desires, Your love remains
Though I stumble, though I falter
Through my weakness, You are strong, Your love
   remains.

"Your Love Remains" by David Gungor and John Arndt
From *CaveTime: The Escape, A Worship Experience*

If fear is cultivated it will become stronger, if faith
is cultivated it will achieve mastery.

—John Paul Jones

Chapter 2

FRAGILE PLACES: *RUNNING TO THE WRONG CAVE*

I remember exactly where I was when I felt distressed for the first time. In fact, it occurred during the same season of life when I made my visit to the ER.

My panic came in two waves, which both came as we happened to be in the process of buying a house. The first one hit while we were on our way to the closing. As we traveled, I began to feel a sense of panic that I'd never felt before. This wave of emotion was a panic worse than what hit me when I thought I was having a heart attack.

I was convinced that something tragic was going to happen to me.

I began to think that I wouldn't be able to make a larger house payment. I was sure I was going to lose my job or my ability to work—and it would be soon. I also thought that I might even die before the first payment.

Yes, the payment was going to be larger, but certainly not large enough to kill anyone! However, when you're distressed, logical thoughts don't necessarily occur to you.

As my mind raced, my heart started beating faster and faster. Before long, I literally couldn't move, so I doubled over. I can't adequately describe the feeling I had as this panic began to mount. But I saw myself vividly having hardship and sickness, and I knew that death would soon come upon me.

You might laugh and say "Come on—it was only a house closing." But the stress of the events and process of my life had brought me to this point, and these feelings and emotions were absolutely real. They were also totally new to me, and I didn't know what to do. I had no doubt that we would not be able to move into our new home and be happy there. I was going to die. Tragedy would strike. It was inevitable.

I felt like a weak little man as I sat there incapacitated. I was inadequate and out of control.

That's when the second wave hit—like a tsunami. Now I began to fret about the home we were selling. I began to feel that something terrible would happen to the people moving into our old home and they would accuse us of hiding it and sue us. They wouldn't just sue us; they would take further legal action against us. We'd found out that the buyers were a staunch Muslim family, and I was convinced that they were going to turn this issue into the next Christians versus Muslims Holy War and attack us. I believed that they were going to stalk us and maybe kill us. To make matters worse, they were on their way to the closing table.

I needed to escape and hide somewhere.

As a pastor, I'm often called to counsel men who find themselves in fragile and frightening spots. Although their situations aren't exactly like mine and the Holy War I was distressed about, their times of distress are every bit as real and intimidating. When this kind of panic comes over you, it can be debilitating and stifling to good judgment and clear thinking.

I find that most of these distressed men are good people. Yet for one reason or another, they find themselves in trouble and believe they have nowhere to go. Many guys stumble at this point. They didn't have an escape plan and have no idea where to hide and collect their thoughts in a healthy fashion.

When we don't know where to go, we can easily make the mistake of escaping to a counterfeit sanctuary. We are running to the wrong cave!

The Three Ds

Someone once said that misery loves company. David had a lot of both! He was attacked relentlessly—pursued and assaulted in every relationship and source of security in his life. He was on the run and looking to hide. However, word got out and 400 men joined him in hiding:

> David left Gath and escaped to the cave of Adullam. When his brothers and his father's household heard about it, they went down to him there. All those who were in distress or in debt or discontented gathered around him, and he became their commander. About four hundred men were with him (1 Samuel 22:1-2).

These men were certainly not a group of model citizens. Nor were they a finely tuned army, at least not yet. Commentator F.B. Meyer describes them as:

> Those who were sorely pressed by misery, poverty, and bitterness of soul...their faces were like the faces of lions...they were swift as roes upon the mountains; but their tempers were probably turbulent and fierce, requiring all the grace and statesmanship of which the young ruler was capable to reduce them to discipline and order.[3]

Regardless of who these men were and why they came to the cave, they were also under assault. We don't know specifically what assaults they faced. But the effects were equally as imminent and potentially just as lethal:

> All those who were in distress or in debt or discontented gathered around him (1 Samuel 22:2).

Author Eugene Peterson describes these men as:

> People whose lives were characterized by debt, distress, and discontent—a congregation of runaways and renegades. It isn't what I would call the cream of the crop of Israelite society. More like dregs from the barrel. Misfits all, it appears. The people who couldn't make it in regular society. Rejects. Losers. Dropouts.[4]

Wow, what a group of vagrants these guys were. All 401 of them escaping from a myriad of assaults, each having his own story and coming to the cave for different reasons.

Some probably believed that Yahweh was on David's side, so an army would amass and dethrone Saul in a mutinous coup. Others might have come as mercenaries. Some wanted women. Others might have been jockeying for a royal position when David became king.[5]

Regardless of their reasons, their stories were different from yours and mine, but in some ways very much the same. The same enemy has been assaulting and attacking men since that fateful day in the Garden. He attacked David through Saul and his death squads. He had specific plans for the 400 others, causing them to run for their lives. Their masculine roles were threatened, and their lives were on the line. Each of them arrived at the cave in some particularly rattled state of being,

I call them the three Ds.

The First D: The State of Distress

The English dictionary defines distress as "a feeling of great pain, anxiety, or sorrow. Acute physical or mental suffering. Affliction. Trouble."[6] However, many Bible commentators agree that the Hebrew term used in 1 Samuel 22 carries an even more acute sense of dire straits, particularly as a result of poverty. This sense of distress would have wide-ranging effects, such as the selling of family members into slavery, the taking of goods and property, and in some extreme cases the taking of a life.[7]

The narrative describes the first portion of David's renegade horde as those who were in distress. Author Cliff Graham describes them as "disgruntled outcasts, emerging from an era in Hebrew history where the worship of Yahweh was almost non-existent."[8] Graham gives us a bit of insight about why these men might have been experiencing extreme distress. They might have been disgruntled warriors who sensed something in David that they respected, believed in, and wanted to follow.

Perhaps they were disgruntled at the fact that the state of their nation was in doubt and God didn't seem to be with them. The military was likely in some sort of disarray as David, one of the most popular commanders ever, had left under a dark cloud.

Many of these men saw Saul as a coward; he had hidden from Goliath. The Spirit of the Lord had left Saul. He possessed no anointing from God, and he wasn't able to lead them bravely in his flesh. Saul's confidence and passion were gone, and his only weapons were fear and intimidation. If a man was disloyal to Saul, he faced certain death. This madman had tried to kill his most trusted bodyguard, David, at least three times; he even tried to take out his own loyal son, Jonathan, once. He certainly wouldn't hesitate to skewer someone else.

Saul was most certainly a demon-possessed coward—a spiritually depraved man. This depraved state made him someone to be feared and fled from. Of course this situation was distressing to these men.

I'm sure many warriors in Saul's kingdom wanted to follow a passionate leader and a giant killer—not someone who had skulked away from a giant. David had shown passion and fearlessness and possessed a magnetism that was otherworldly.

Saul was no real leader at all, but David was. Without a doubt, David was God's man in their eyes.

But now he was gone, and he had left under a cloud of suspicion. Panic, anxiety, and the effects of distress set in for some of these warriors as they realized that there was no leader for them to follow. And the one they would follow had either been chased out of town or had fled—they didn't know for sure.

Just as I experienced in my time of distress, the sweating and nausea would come in waves during the daytime, and their minds would be hounded by visions of impending death at night. This meant little or no sleep.

They needed a leader to show them the way out of this anguish. Their panic assaulted them in their minds so vividly that their bodies felt as if it were real. They needed a real leader, and the man for the job was David. But he had escaped and was now in hiding.

The answer? These men decided to escape and hide with him. He would know how to lead them.

Reed, Sarah, and the wrong cave. Reed was a good man. He'd been faithful to his wife, Sarah, and was a committed father to his three sons.

Reed had worked quietly at the same job for twenty-five years, but his company was going bankrupt. He was in jeopardy of losing his retirement and everything he'd worked for. He was also becoming distant and short-tempered with Sarah and the boys. During this time, Sarah called me and said, "Pastor Jeff, Reed is drawing away from me and I feel as if I am losing him. He won't talk to me. He won't open up anymore and he's distant. I even think that there might be someone else."

When I asked why she thought Reed was interested in another woman, she said that she'd caught him on the computer on a social networking site. He was reading a personal message he'd received from a former girlfriend. The letter was about a project taking place to benefit their old high school, sponsored by alumni who used to be student council members with Reed. The woman said because they had been student council members together, she thought he might want to get involved in the project. The words that alarmed Sarah were: "It could be like old times."

Whether or not Reed was really thinking of cheating on Sarah, I'm glad she caught him. At the very least, Reed was contemplating going to the wrong cave.

What's the wrong cave? The wrong cave is a place where we try to escape everything that is actually happening in our lives. We just hide. In the wrong cave, there's no focus on being with God and getting the hole inside us filled by Him. In the wrong cave, we just try to hide and we attempt to fill the hole with something or someone else other than God.

When David escaped to the cave, he wanted to get out of Saul's target range and hear from his close and personal God about what he should do. However, Reed was contemplating helping his old girl-friend, and he had even responded back to her a couple of times to inquire in more detail about the project. Reed was running to the wrong cave because he was hiding something questionable. This kind of hiding has nothing to do with God. Wrong cave. Wrong motive.

In fact, Reed later admitted to me that when he did interact with this old girlfriend, he felt a slight sense of excitement whenever he clicked the send button on the computer screen. They'd had a great relationship in high school, and by the look of her picture on her profile, she'd aged quite well.

He also felt strangely excited that Sarah didn't know what he was doing. For that matter, he technically wasn't doing anything wrong. It was all innocent and platonic, he thought. But Reed was at least approaching the entrance of the wrong cave. He was thinking about hiding in the wrong cave of an old relationship that made him feel young again. But any cave that would lead to spending time alone with a woman other than his wife was definitely the wrong cave.

As Reed and I talked about this situation, I learned that he was distressed about his job being terminated. He also hadn't been feeling very fulfilled in his life lately. He was feeling old, worn out, and not passionate about much in his life. While he might not have used this language, he had a hole inside of him that he was trying to fill with another person and a fantasy of what once was. The old flame contacting him was an invitation, he thought, to feel some passion again and be pursued.

This cave seemed to offer the allure of the old feelings of youth, and it was a welcome distraction from the reality of what seemed like a dull and monotonous life. However, in reality, this cave offered to Reed the potential of an emotional affair and possibly a full-blown adulterous rendezvous. I thank God that Reed got caught heading toward the wrong cave.

I'm happy to report that Reed and Sarah had a deep talk, shed a few tears together, and their hearts began to be pointed back toward each other.

Instead of running to the wrong cave, Reed stepped into his masculine roles. In Role 1, he went to God alone, asking for help and affirmation that he could only get from His Creator. He allowed God to fill the hole inside. He then stepped into Role 2 as he exercised his masculine presence and took the website off of his computer and took measures to make sure that it would not happen in his home again. He then stepped into Role 3 and entered into community with his wife by being transparent and vulnerable. He also got recommitted to a group of guys who met weekly for CaveTime, telling them of his temptation toward the other cave, asking them to help him stay away from ever going there again.

These men would be a wall for him, and he would once again be a wall for Sarah and his sons.

Are you running to the wrong cave? Have you ever escaped and tried to hide in the wrong cave? I have. In fact, it was the one that landed me in the ER and the ensuing Holy War that I had imagined at the closing table.

For me, the wrong cave was performance. I was addicted to performing and being competitive in most of the areas of my life, and eventually I lost control. I competed for God's love and acceptance by doing as many religious things as I could—and doing them well, I might add. I was intent on having the most obedient children (and I am sad to say, my motivation was because their behavior was a reflection on whether I was a good parent or not).

Performance. It was all about me. I was also intent on having a great marriage, and if my wife Lori would just fit in and do what a good pastor's wife was supposed to, people would think well of me—I mean us. Performance, yet again.

Who knows why I ended up this way! But it was all about me, including me heading to the wrong cave. I performed to feel significant and to fill the hole inside with deeds and accomplishments that pointed to me. I was Super Jeff. Well, Super Jeff was in an ER and needed some counseling. But there God was, whispering to me. In my distress, God was calling me to the cave.

When a man wants to know God—and I really did—God won't let him go on forever in the wrong way, ending up in the wrong cave. Through the darkness and pain, God will draw us to the cave, so that we might hide together with Him.

And yes, assaults will come again and we'll make mistakes. We will temporarily take other paths again. But once the temporarily misguided man glances back toward the grace-worn path to the cave, even hinting that he wants to come home, God is there.

God reads much into the pained and longing-for-grace-again glances of men. These are glances that motivate Him, faster than the speed of sound, to bum-rush and bowl us over like a grace-filled tsunami—one that's like Tigger pouncing on Pooh. Like a faithful canine waiting at the front window for his long-gone master to return—kissing him, pouncing on him, and dancing a dance of hope and joy. That giant-killing dance that fills the hole of distress with the hope-giving life of God within a man.

The Second D: The State of Debt

The average debt in most American homes accumulates with interest rates so exorbitant that the sum will never be repaid. This ugly financial heap looms like a mountain on the horizon. And it is so imposing that bankruptcies occur at an alarming rate. This is exemplified by the following report, which cites rising bankruptcy filings from 2006-2010. With the current economic straits, there seems to be no end in sight:

> Personal bankruptcy filings rose to their highest levels on record, with estimates in excess of 2 million filings. According to Lundquist Consulting, a research company based in California, there were 115,000 bankruptcy filings in November 2010. Year-to-date, there were 9 percent more bankruptcy filings by November 2010 compared to that same timeframe a year earlier. Nationally, there were roughly 6,000 bankruptcy filings per million individuals, or 1 in every 160 people.[9]

This is staggering. Not only does this type of debt leave people's bank accounts in poor health, it can adversely affect both physical and mental health as well. Depression, anxiety, digestive tract issues, migraine headaches, and ulcers are just some of the confirmed effects of adverse stress-related issues caused as a result of debt.[10] Piling on, nearly one-third of states now allow creditors to sue individuals for defaulting on their debts, sending them to prison if they can't pay.[11] While debtor's prison was officially outlawed in 1833, this is certainly a modern-day form of it and can bring a huge amount of stress to bear on any man who is trying to provide for and be a wall to his family.

Currently many men in our society can't pay their debts and don't know what to do. They might run to the wrong caves or maybe they just try to run aimlessly and not pay. They constantly look over their shoulder for the repo man and dodge phone calls because of the debt collectors' repeated calls.

Assaulted and chased. I'm sure that these men could commiserate with David's 400 as they escaped the debt collectors' henchmen and hid deep in the cave at Adullam.

Sean, Linda, and the absence of a fairy tale. Sean was a guy who came to me and was living out the story of the men who showed up at the cave, running from their debts. He was a recovering addict who had met his wife, Linda, while they were both in the same recovery program. Both of them had found the Lord while they were in treatment, and the structure, transparency, and accountability offered in recovery was ideal for them.

They married soon after their graduation ceremony and started what they hoped would be a happy and peaceful life together. In addition to being a talented computer programmer, Sean was very entrepreneurial. Linda got pregnant with their first son soon after the wedding, and Sean got busy starting his first company. As the Internet continued to explode, Sean dreamed about and developed new products, and the money began to flow. Within another year, Linda was pregnant with their second son. Sean began to feel the pressures of a rapidly growing business, family, and the need to perform to keep up with the demands coming at him from every direction.

Sean had the same root addiction that I had, the need to perform. But as a recovering addict, he also had some other addictions as well. Addictions to cocaine and prostitution had plagued him in the past, and with the demands in his life, he found himself beginning to wrestle with them again. As the pressure began to assault and chase him, Sean had no frame of reference for how or where to escape and hide so that he might hear from God. He didn't know that God was with him, ready at any instant to pounce on him and smother him with grace.

When I met Sean, I had no idea all of this was going on in his life. He and Linda had recently come to our church and were referred to me for counseling by another pastor on staff. I invited Sean to come to a CaveTime that I was having at my house. He began to show up and just "be" with a band of men who would be his brothers, sharing his story of addiction with them and not being judged.

There's no judgment in the cave—only accountability, grace, and more grace. Our motto is: "What's said in the cave stays in the cave." Sean certainly needed transparency with the security of confidentiality. He began to listen to the Scriptures we read together, with men worshipping quietly and then praying for each other's stuff. He also began to hear those same men pray for their wives and their children, and his wife and his children, and whatever else needed to be given to God there in the cave.

I wish that I could say that everything got better and that we all lived happily ever after. But that's not what happened. The guys in the cave were unaware, but in addition to his being assaulted by addiction, Sean had incurred some debts that were almost insurmountable. He was being chased by debt collectors, clients he wasn't servicing, and some unsavory characters who wanted to do him some great bodily harm. He began running to the wrong caves, ones that were familiar to him. He ran to other women to try and ease the pain. He ran to cocaine to try and get a quick buzz that might help him forget. And he began to drink pretty heavily, too.

While Sean was running and trying to hide, Linda was at home with two sons and pregnant with a third. She had no food, no diapers, and no money to pay the bills. Sean would leave for days at a time and not tell anyone.

On one occasion, when he did come home, he was rightfully questioned rather passionately by Linda. Her questions angered Sean, he got physical with her, and the police were called. Because Sean had been in trouble before and was a convicted felon, he was taken to jail. He and I had CaveTime there, except this time he was wearing an orange jumpsuit and there was a glass window in between us. Yet God was there with us.

I read Sean Scripture over the telephone receiver, prayed for him—and then I got in his face. I told him that he wasn't being a wall for his wife and his sons, and he was in jeopardy of losing them and everything that he loved. I asked him why he allowed himself to get to this point and he said, "I just didn't know what to do as the debts mounted. I didn't want to upset the guys in the cave, and I was being chased by all kinds of folks who wanted their money and the services that they had paid for. I wasn't able to pay them, so I ran to what I had known in the past."

When Lori and I moved away from that city, Sean was still running to the wrong caves, and Linda was in the process of trying to start a new life without him.

I know this isn't a success story. But it does show the power of fear and debt, the relentless pursuit of a nasty enemy, and the danger of hiding in the wrong caves.

The guys hiding with David in the cave must have had some pretty significant debts to cause them to flee as they did. In David's day, many people incurred debts, just as people do today. But the Hebrew word describing these men referred to a *bad* debt—one that was very late and was in serious default. This was the kind of debt that prompted someone to try to collect their money, or goods, or something—and it was going to happen *today!*[12]

During David's era, those who owed debt were also likely to receive all kinds of punishment from their creditors. A creditor could take property, family members, or even inflict severe bodily harm. Some of us know the pressure of collection calls, but thankfully we don't live in a culture where one of our offspring could be taken as payment on a debt.

Maybe you're a young man and think you are immune to incurring such a deep level of indebtedness. Think again. The debt load carried by many college students is staggering. Currently, two-thirds of all college students carry some type of debt to finance their education, with the total amount borrowed in 2008-2009 being $75.1 billion. This was a dramatic 25 percent increase over the amount in the previous year.[13] These types of debt loads make it almost impossible for many young men to finish their education and make ends meet. It has become such a problem that an increasing number of students are leaving the country and/or just not paying back their loans.[14] As if student loan debt isn't bad enough, in addition to these mounting debts, the average college-aged undergraduate is also amassing a sizable credit card balance that has increased 41 percent in the last seven years to $3,200.[15]

Student loan and credit card debt plague and assault many young men with a pressure that is sizable and stressful. The pressure can drive them to the wrong caves. Young men, middle-aged men, and older men all have their own types of financial struggles and assaults that weigh on them and cause stress. Stress can make men of any age want to run! It can make us want to hide and feel as if we must escape to someplace.

Broken and fearful. Ragged and torn. God is calling all men, in all conditions, to escape. Escape to the right cave, where He will be with you.

The Third D: The State of Discontentment

Some of the men who met David at the cave were in debt and some were distressed. But probably all of them were discontented. The Hebrew word for discontent is *mar*, which means "to make bitter"; it also describes "the heart-crushing experience of family turmoil, impending death, or an unfulfilled death wish."[16] This kind of discontentment reaches right into the very soul of a man and wrenches him in his guts.

Interestingly, this meaning paints quite a picture of the person experiencing discontentment. David's guys fit every aspect of this definition. They really had no future within their culture. They were bitter. They owed vast amounts of money to people who sought to collect their payment in property or in flesh. With a growing list of failures, these guys might have left behind families who were frustrated and actually thankful for their absence. Some might have left out of disdain for the evil monarch who was chasing David, and they wanted to go down fighting on the side of the giant killer in hiding.

These men were hanging on by their fingernails. They ran to hide, to collect their thoughts, to write their wills, and to do whatever desperate men do before life as they know it comes to an end. All in all, these guys had decided that if they were going to go down, they were going to go down swinging with David, their leader and "commander":

> All those who were in distress or in debt or discontented gath-ered around him, and he became their commander. About four hundred men were with him (1 Samuel 22:2).

The word for commander in 1 Samuel is an interesting term because it carries with it a sense of royalty or nobility. The word means much more than they took a vote and made him their leader. It means that they saw something in him. They sensed something on him.

I'm sure many had heard about Samuel anointing David years before. Others had seen him kill Goliath and knew that he had an uncanny and supernatural presence about him. And some might have just sensed that David was different. But these men realized they were at a crossroads in their lives. In the midst of all of their Ds—because of all their Ds—they had to be with this guy.

David was their king. They were in the right cave, no doubt about it. He had followed the leading of his God, in spite of his brokenness, to a place of hiding and darkness.

At this point in history, the worship of Yahweh had grown cold, and David's relationship with Him was unique. David knew God. David walked with God in a place of powerful fire, passionate tears, and relentless love. This must have been something that at the very least incited a deep curiosity in the 400. When they came to a place of despondency, they were drawn to the real king who had the real fire given to him by God.

Perhaps the real king would hear from God and save them from the assaults being waged upon them. The feeling that they got in their despondent and wrenched guts was that this was the right commander and the right cave. As David followed his Commander to the cave, these men followed theirs.

Real God. Real cave. Safe cave. It had to be, or they were dead men—401 dead men.

Lord, save me now, for my heart is weary
Darkness surrounds and my spirit's breaking
Come save me now Almighty, my strength alone
  is nothing,
come show Your power in me, I find my hope in
  You.
You are my, You are my, You are my refuge
Come save me now Almighty, my strength alone
  is nothing, come show Your power in me, I
  find my hope in You, my hope in You alone

"Save Me Now" by David Gungor and John Arndt
From *CaveTime: A Worship Experience*

At eighteen our convictions are the hills from
which we look; at forty-five, they are the caves in
which we hide.

—F. Scott Fitzgerald

Chapter 3

SAVE ME NOW: *LIFE GETS MESSY!*

When I was young, I thought that I had most of life's big issues figured out. I was above it all, resting high on my self-constructed hill of youthful arrogance and performance, with its accompanying cycle of reward and punishment.

When I performed well, things were good between me, God, and the people around me. My mantra: "Just do good and get blessed." When I didn't perform so well—which wasn't all that often—things weren't so peachy. I guess I subconsciously had another mantra: "Do bad, get punished."

I also forced heaven and hell into this system. Good people (of whom I was one) went to heaven, while bad people, well, they went to the other place. I could neatly categorize and see this system as I sat on my hill. Seeing how I could please God with my well-lived life and stay in His good graces seemed obvious from my hilltop perch.

Over the years—and after the culmination of being confronted with my own emotional, spiritual, and physical weaknesses—being up on that hill seemed to make me more of a target. Instead of being above it all, I could no longer ignore the regular assaults coming my way. I thought these kinds of attacks only happened to people who didn't have their stuff together. Either my assumption wasn't true, or I didn't have my stuff together. Or maybe both.

Or maybe assaults were part of every man's life and that didn't necessarily have anything to do with performance or God's favor. If this was true, I needed to get off of my hill immediately, find some cover, and get a new strategy. Instead of sitting on top of my hill, I needed to go and hide inside it. But how?

Cave-Struck

In the hospital ER and over the next couple of years, I discovered that life gets messy. It certainly wasn't as neat, tidy, and tight as I wanted it to be. I also found that I couldn't control events and people and perform well enough to fill the hole inside of me. Instead of filling that hole with my own arrogance and ignorance, I needed to find a place that was out of the line of fire and the harmful elements that strike people who sit on hilltops.

A cave maybe?

The prophet Elijah heard the voice of the Lord in a cave. The philosopher Plato spoke of his cave in his classic work, *The Republic*. The Desert Fathers and Mothers lived in them and saw visions of angels and demons there. Batman has one called the Bat Cave, and Superman retreats to his, which he calls the Fortress of Solitude. We're in some famous company when we speak of caves. But until my mid-twenties, I'd never even been in one. When I finally did enter my first cave, it left an indelible impression on me.

On the day of my first real cave experience, I didn't even think to check the weather. It just wasn't that important to me. Regardless of the weather conditions, I was going fishing and nothing could keep me from it. Fishing has a mesmerizing effect upon many men, causing them to avoid all rationality and clear thinking. This irrational behavior and inability to think clearly—especially when pertaining to trout—came over me when I was a young boy and has plagued me ever since. It can cloud clear judgment and cause even the strongest and most disciplined men to do silly things and take crazy risks.

On this particular day, the pursuit of the elusive trout had once again blurred my vision, drawing me into an angling vortex, and I was powerless to fight it. The only way to deal with it was to give in. I *had* to fish.

At that time in my life, my frequent partner in angling crime was my father. We were particularly excited that day because my friend Kyle and I had camped and fished at a particular spot a couple of years earlier, and we had found it to be amazingly beautiful. The spot was Lincoln Lake, a high-mountain lake that was very deep and showed great promise for big fish. The lake was situated in a sheer rock bowl, just behind the summit of the 14,230-foot Mount Evans. Dad and I had been talking about going there for a while. And it was now going to happen.

Heigh-Ho Bullet!

The night before the excursion I had a tough time sleeping, with dreams of big fish and many of them. Morning finally came and Dad picked me up in the old blue Subaru named "Bullet" (for the rust spots that looked like an M-16 had opened fire on the back end of it). We headed west, talking, laughing, and telling fish stories.

To access this spot, Dad parked Bullet on a little patch of gravel at the edge of one of the highest mountain roads in the nation. We literally parked and then walked in the clouds. After an hour of sliding down an extremely steep slope, upsetting a family of mountain goats, and sinking in alpine tundra, we rounded a sheer rock bowl on the back side of Mount Evans.

As we descended out of the clouds, we found ourselves on the east edge of Lincoln Lake. The view was breathtaking, scary, ominous, eerie, rugged, and indescribably beautiful. It reminded me of C.S. Lewis' quote that God "isn't safe. But he's good."[17] These mountains were more beautiful than anything I'd ever seen, but equally as rugged and certainly not safe.

Those who have fished and hunted with me know that I am gifted when it comes to getting my line, fly, or decoys into the water when wild game is at stake. This day was no different. Within minutes of coming out of those clouds, I had a black gnat tied to a two-pound test leader, threaded through a clear bubble, filled with water and then, "bzzzzzzzzzz, plop," my fly was working its mojo. Within just seconds of that fly hitting the water, *boom,* a beautiful brook trout hit my fly and it was on. Hmmm, I did think that I might have also heard a slight boom of thunder. But again, when you have fishing fever, these things don't register clearly.

Within a couple of minutes, I had the trout on a stringer, my fly dried out, and "bzzzzzzzzzz, plop," I was back on the water.

As a bit of a side note, those who have fished or hunted with my dad know that he is the opposite of me when it comes to pursuing both winged and finned prey. In lay terms, he's as slow as molasses at getting his fly or decoys on the water. He arranges and rearranges, ties slowly, and then calls on the powers of heaven to take a vote and write it in the clouds for him. On that day as we fished in those clouds, Dad's ritual was no different.

Ignoring the Signs

Dad had just heard from heaven, chosen a fly, and was starting to get his leader material out of his tackle box. *Boom,* another fish hit my fly—another feisty brookie a bit larger than the first one. My heart was racing and my predator instinct was totally out of control. Looking back, I know I was out of control because I indeed did hear peals of thunder and see flashes of lightning. But I was powerless to take evasive action—the fishing was just too good!

Because I'd grown up in Colorado, I should have had the sense to process what I knew in my head. The mountains are beautiful, but they can be every bit as treacherous. When weather moves in at altitude, you need to take cover. Now! But I was looney with the powerful angling sickness as that second brookie fought me. What's more, the process of casting and immediately catching a fish happened four more times, and my insanity continued to spin out of control.

I was brought back to the sane world by Dad, however, when he yelled over the wind and now rain mixed with hail, "Jeff, that's lightning. It's really close…on top of us. We have to go, *now!*"

I thought that he was just jealous and lying to me because he hadn't caught a single fish. But he was deadly serious. In my fishing frenzy, I had ignored the signs of an impending storm. We were stuck, with a very high probability of being struck.

It's difficult to describe the feeling of total helplessness that we felt as we realized that this storm had set in on us within thirty minutes of starting to fish. Because of our position in that rock bowl, below the summit of Mount Evans, we couldn't see the storm coming very far in advance. That lack of vision, coupled with ignoring all signs and sounds of bad weather, meant we were really in trouble.

I'm not exaggerating, as numerous people die each year in the mountains as a result of lightning strikes. The vast majority of them are males, involved in outdoor activities in the summer months.[18]

Dad and I were candidates on all counts.

We realized we had to get out of there as quickly as possible or risk death. Lightning was striking all around us, as well as in the clouds above us where Bullet was parked. We needed to escape and hide. But where?

As we tried to make our way through the rain and hail and back up the steep, wet, and very cold rocks, I saw what looked like a hole in the side of the mountain between two boulders. We made our way toward the opening, and suddenly there it was—a real, bona fide cave.

I had never been so happy in my life to see something that was dank, musty, and dark. But those characteristics didn't matter at all because it was pretty dry and out of the life-threatening elements. It was a door out of the storm and into the mountain—a shelter from a potentially deadly force.

An escape. A hiding place. We found a cave of refuge that day.

A Life of Extremes

Within forty-five minutes, the storm had passed. The sun came out and we obviously didn't die. That's life in the Rockies. Extremes. Extremely beautiful and extremely dangerous.

Life can be like that as well, can't it? As I reflect back on that particular situation, I realize that I completely ignored all signs of the impending storm. In my ignorance, I made at least three major mistakes.

First, I didn't check the weather report the night before. I should have. This might have cued me to be watching and listening for signs of danger.

Second, once the signs of the approaching storm hinted that trouble was on its way, I didn't pay much attention. I was totally distracted by the fishing frenzy. I realize now that even the way the fish were feeding was a sign of possible storms. As a result of the change in barometric pressure, wild game are prone to feed in crazy fashion before a storm. All the warning signals for a dangerous mountain storm were screaming at me, way before my dad did.

Third, Dad tried to warn me before I really paid attention to him. But I ignored him as well. I thought to myself, "Sure he wants to leave, I am kicking his butt. I am in the zone!"

What's more, I hadn't noticed the cave before. We had walked right by it. The cave was there the whole time. I just didn't take time to look for it on our trip in because I was so focused on getting my line in the water first. I was distracted by my competitive nature to get in the water before Dad and to catch more fish than he did.

Performance and competition—a dangerous combination in the wrong context.

Early Warning Signs

I can't help but think that David had some early warning signs, before his life got dangerous, that assault was coming his way. Saul must have made a snide remark or two about one of those songs that made David out to be more of a war hero than himself.

Maybe David was too caught up in everything going on in his life. After all, he had been a nobody tending sheep. Then almost overnight, with the whole Goliath episode, David became quite the living legend. He had no taxes to pay, he was married to the king's daughter, and he got to hang out at the palace. Life was very good and very successful. It had to be fun and fulfilling:

> In everything he did he had great success, because the LORD was with him (1 Samuel 18:14).

Temper tantrums and dark clouds and thunder. Success can be intoxicating, fun, and at times, exhilarating. Unfortunately, it can also blur your vision to what's coming right at you. I think that this might be what happened to David.

Saul obviously had some serious anger issues. He took the art of the temper tantrum to a new level. His tantrums fueled a rage in him toward David that finally exploded, to the point that Saul hurled a spear at David's face and the red hair that sat on top of it. Several times.

The key phrase here is "fueled a rage." Saul couldn't have started with the spear throwing. Yelling, cursing, and throwing other things probably preceded the spears. There had to be black clouds on the horizon before the storm hit.

Was life so good that David just didn't see that first spear attack until he was in the middle of it? Kind of like a guy in the middle of a fishing frenzy, who ignores thunder, more thunder, and then lightning strikes, only to end up in a potentially lethal storm.

David found himself in a lethal storm.

I know that I was just on a fishing trip and David was being threatened by a king. But the core mistakes seem comparable to me. There were definitely hints for me that day that a lighting storm was about to set in.

For example, a meteorologist could have clued me in and warned me the night before, if only I had turned on the local news. What would have happened had David consulted the prophet Samuel, the spiritual newscaster of his day, about Saul's rage? Would he have been able to avert some of the events that took place?

Maybe I should have consulted someone about the emptiness and anxiety that I was feeling before a full-blown panic attack, accompanied by heart attack symptoms. Of course, I had a reputation to keep and didn't want anyone to see my weaknesses. I'd rather continue to try and sit upon the hill of my convictions. Remember? I had the conviction that life was a competition for me—a competition to prove myself in as many arenas as I could. I was going to win. Crazy, isn't it?

Still, there were some early warning signs for me. Signposts pointing to an ER and a counselor's office. Thunder clouds in the distance. Another was the sinking feeling in the pit of my stomach that just stayed there. I didn't know why it was there. I now know that my emotions just got stuck on competition mode, so my body decided to stay nervous.

Another warning sign: I was only able to sleep a couple of hours at night before waking up in a cold sweat. I now realize this was another symptom of my body staying ready for competition and the need to perform and prove myself. Thunder clouds again. My sleeplessness was the result of that hole in me that was longing to be filled.

I ignored these warning signs until I couldn't any longer. Tension and nervousness seemed to be my constant companions. I learned to mask them with activity, then doing more, often in the name of God. I only felt good if the activities I was involved in grew bigger and better. Physically, I only felt good about my body if I ran marathons, attempted 100-mile races, had the heaviest backpack on our yearly trip, or lifted more than anyone in the weight room. I could only rest after proving myself again and again and again. And even then, rest occurred only for short periods of time. No real rest. No peace.

Posing. False success. False results. A false sense of security.

Thunder clouds were rolling in on me over a period of years, lightning was on the horizon, and I was caught in a frenzy of fishing activity, trying to fill the hole.

Places of refuge. One thing that David had going for him was a series of caves that he knew well. Scripture tells us that he knew the caves in several regions near the place where he grew up, and he went to them often. He probably discovered these hideaways as he tended his father's sheep.

At least when David's assault came his way, he had caves in mind. On the day of my fishing trip, I didn't even have a clue that a cave existed nearby. No escape route or plan. That could have been tragic on a day that was supposed to be fun.

Even in my fun I had to compete. This mindset blurred my reasoning to check for an escape route and a possible place to hide. I had no physical cave on that day in the clouds, nor did I have a spiritual one in my life either.

David spoke of his cave:

> I love you, O LORD my strength. The LORD is my rock, my fortress and my deliverer; my God is my rock, in whom I take refuge (Psalm 18:1-2).

God was David's rock, his cave. Yes, we've explored how he escaped to a physical cave at a place called Adullam. But the cave was just a physical place where he would take time to really get with The Cave: God. When David hid in his cave, he was taking refuge in his God. CaveTime was a time to escape, show up, and get covered and hidden by the only One who could cover and hide a man like he needed to be hidden.

Hidden by God. In the cave. By The Cave.

Several terms in Psalm 18 give amazing insight into how David saw God as his Cave.

In verse 1, David tells God that he loves Him. The term David uses for "love" was usually used between a mother and her child. It speaks of tender love expressed over a long period of time. David ran to the cave in Adullam in order to be hidden in God's love. David's love for God had also been growing deeper over time. He didn't just start to have CaveTime on the day that he escaped to the cave at Adullam.

In verse 2 we find the term "rock," which gives us additional insight about how David saw God as his Cave. David used this word to express that God is faithful, consistent, and immovable, throughout the generations. The love between David and his God was founded upon God's consistency, throughout all generations and in all circumstances. David's CaveTime, then, was a time where he would be hidden and cared for by the Eternal One. In the cave, they would deal with the assaults together. David would be getting assistance from the One who would faithfully stand with him always.

Also in verse 2, we find the term "refuge." This term described a high place in a mountainous region where the natural topography made it impenetrable. David's CaveTime was built on the foundation of showing up for a time in the cave with the Cave whom David loved deeply. God would provide refuge by covering David, taking him at any time, any place, and in any condition and setting him up high. CaveTime sets a man up high and provides safety and perspective that no one else and no other place can provide.[19]

David was under assault, being chased relentlessly. For all we know, he had done nothing overtly wrong. What was David thinking? Was God attacking him? Was it the devil? Was it God using the devil? David didn't have much time to sit and debate the issues. If he did, he risked becoming "the late David." There was no doubt in his mind he had to find a cave

What about You?

Can you relate to David? Or can you relate to me up in the mountains?

Maybe you've overlooked some warning signs in your life and a storm has set in on you. Lightning is striking all around and you are stuck. Or maybe you feel as if you are being hotly pursued by someone or something and have no idea what you've done wrong. Maybe you've lost a job for no obvious reason. Maybe you feel as if you've lost everything. Maybe you *have* lost everything.

These types of losses and questions can cause you to doubt yourself and your abilities. They can cause you to doubt God's love for you or even to doubt His very existence. Over an extended period of time, these doubts and stresses can bring about depression, anxiety, and relational strain. They can distance you from God. These thunder clouds on the horizon and temper tantrums thrown by crazed monarchs are signs of impending storms and spears coming your way.

You might be distressed as you stumble and wallow helplessly in your relationship with your wife. Maybe you are disconnected with your kids. Distant from God.

The fires of lust burn in all of us, and sexually deviant practices are fueled by easy access to porn via the Internet. The war room of hell has easy access to our homes. Thunder rolls and lightning strikes all around us. We hear the footsteps of Saul's hit men. What will we do?

All men are targets. Our sexuality, self-image, and self-worth are shaken and assaulted relentlessly. Scores and scores of men, trying to escape to the wrong kinds of caves. We seek pleasure and self-indulgence to numb the pain of what our real lives have become.

David speaks for himself, for the 400 who were with him, for me, and maybe for all men as he crosses the threshold of the cave there in Adullam:

> Have mercy on me, my God, have mercy on me, for in you
> I take refuge. I will take refuge in the shadow of your wings
> until the disaster has passed (Psalm 57:1-5).

What a relief! The Cave. A spiritual hiding place until the storms pass and the dangers subside.

God is the Ultimate Cave—the One in whom we hide. Our Refuge. Our Fortress. He is the One who will calm the storms and confront the murderous hit men sent by the Evil One.

Come with me now and we'll explore what happens in the cave, with The Cave.

Lord, my shepherd strong
I shall not want, You lead me to pastures
To quiet waters,
Restore my soul.
And though I walk through death's own shadow
I fear no evil, Thy rod and staff, they comfort me.

"Shepherd Strong" by David Gungor and John Arndt
From *CaveTime: The Escape, A Worship Experience*

Manhood is the social barrier that societies must erect against entropy, human enemies, the forces of nature, time, and all the human weaknesses that endanger group life.

—David D. Gilmore

Chapter 4

ROLE ASSAULT: *THE ENEMY'S SUBVERSIVE STRATEGY*

I'd describe Zane as a highly motivated performance addict. It takes one to know one, right? He came to me one day and said he had heard me speak about my journey to the cave and some of the symptoms I experienced during that time in my life.

He simply said, "That's where I am right now."

He described how he wasn't sleeping. He had an almost insatiable desire to grow his company, and he couldn't stop thinking about it. Business was booming and almost racing out of control, and so were his mind and his emotions. He was feeling panic and dread.

Can you say thunder clouds?

Zane realized that these feelings weren't healthy, but he wasn't sure what to do. "What do you recommend?" he said with a sullen look on his face.

Of course, you can guess that I urged him to start having a regular CaveTime. I also encouraged him to meet with a brother or brothers who would allow him to be totally transparent without judging him. Finally, I told Zane that in order to deal with what he was facing, he had to allow God to speak to him about his priorities.

How did it work out for Zane? Here's what his wife, Jill, said via an email I received on our CaveTime.org website.

Jeff: I want to thank you for the *CaveTime* concept and how it's affected my husband. I've noticed a remarkable change in him, specifically in the areas of his quiet time and getting to a place of being vocal about his stress level and turning it all over to God. He is a mighty force, that one, and seeing him leading our little family and stepping up to lead in other ways is pretty stinkin' amazing. Thanks for your leadership. In fact, we're in the office right now and he is playing the *CaveTime* worship CD…wowzers. Unbelievable.

That's what it is all about. Zane's wife had seen real, life-altering change.

Relentless

The enemy has a strategy, and it involves assaulting men relentlessly. If Satan can effectively attack men, then he might get them out of their roles. If he succeeds, things will begin to crumble. Of course, his strategy is deceiving. Sometimes he hits us when we're down. Remember Reed and his temptation with an old high school flame or Sean and his overwhelming struggle with debt? But the enemy can also hit in places that don't seem inherently bad—such as when we're performing for the Lord as I have done, or when business is booming and wildly successful as it was for Zane.

When we boil them down to basics, the enemy's assaults on the 401 there in the cave—and for that matter on every man—are direct attacks on the very essence of masculinity. Satan attacks the three roles we looked at in the Introduction.

In this chapter, I want to take one last look at the condition David and his men were in when they arrived at the entrance of the cave. I also want you to see how some of the men I've come in contact with through the years have entered the cave as well. Then, in the next chapter, we'll look at what happens to men when they spend time in the cave and why CaveTime can be such a life-altering occurrence.

When we're attacked to the point that we can't function in our roles, we begin to crumble as men. If we don't escape and get help with understanding and functioning in these roles, our masculinity disintegrates. Our marriages fall apart. Our homes deteriorate. Our churches weaken. Our cities collapse. And our perception of ourselves dissolves.

The men who arrived at the cave were living examples of the effectiveness of the enemy's strategy. Their lives were crumbling and they desperately needed help. During this time in Israel, men didn't know or seek God as they had in the past.[20] That's a significant part of why David stood out so intensely. He did seek God. He knew God. God was with him. Perhaps David didn't know why he faced Saul's attacks, and maybe his life didn't make sense. But he knew God would speak to him. So David crossed the threshold of the cave, intent on hiding with God and trying to make sense of what was going on in his life.

Assault on Role 1

David eventually understood Role 1. Remember this role? It involves pursuing an individual relationship with God first.

God was with David, and he realized that. He also knew where to go when he was assaulted. He knew he needed some extended CaveTime. Eventually. Eventually, David knew all of this. However, the cave wasn't the first place David headed when things started to crumble in his life.

Here's the route that David took to get to the cave. It certainly wasn't the most direct! He stopped by his house (1 Samuel 19:11), his mentor's house (1 Samuel 19:18), his friend Jonathan's house (1 Samuel 20:1), the church for food and a weapon (1 Samuel 21:1), to Gath in an effort to intimidate old enemies (1 Samuel 21:10), and then finally to the cave (1 Samuel 22:1).

At the cave, David would hear from the One who had made him a man, had him anointed king, and had apparently allowed him to be in his current situation. In David's own words, Role 1 came to life as he described what he'd be doing in the cave:

Until I learn what God will do for me (1 Samuel 22:3).

Although David made a lot of stops before he got to the cave to be with God, once he arrived he knew he was there to learn what God would do for him. No doubt about it, God would speak to him. David just needed to show up and listen.

Maybe God was showing David that real hiding can't take place anywhere else. Real hiding only happens in the cave, with The Cave. We can learn from David and just go to the cave first!

I believe the men who followed David to the cave sensed that he had an inside track with God. They believed it to such a degree that they were willing to risk their lives. The enemy's assaults eventually drove these men to the threshold of the cave as well. And with David, they would learn how to seek God first.

Zane's trip to the cave. At the beginning of this chapter I told you about Zane who caught on to the importance of CaveTime. When he asked me what to do, I remember that I urged him to go to God first. Role 1 is number one for a reason. God must be first.

In the next chapter, we'll examine the nuts and bolts of CaveTime. But I think it's important to stress that CaveTime isn't easy. Zane didn't change effortlessly or instantly—it took a significant period of time for changes to occur in his life. But the starting point for him— and for any man who enters the cave—is to have individual CaveTime with God first.

Zane understood that Role 1 was eroding in his life. He saw the thunder clouds and lightning in the distance. Fortunately, he didn't just keep fishing in a frenzy of activity. He did something about it. He escaped and arrived at the cave, and there Zane gave God His rightful place and began to seek Him.

Zane was no different than the 401 men at Adullam. We've looked at the assaults they faced. They owed people huge sums of money. They were caught up in a political tug of war between two kings, and they were distressed and despondent because of it.

It's vital that we see what was taking place in their lives and what is going on in our lives today: *an assault on Role 1.* The enemy doesn't want men to escape and hide with their God. Why? Because God will help them. He'll instruct them, repair them, and change them. He is the only One who can do this.

Assault on Role 2

David also understood Role 2: God created him to be a masculine presence, on behalf of God, for the people in his world.

David certainly was quite a masculine presence as he was hacking off Goliath's huge head. He was again when he went to war and defended his nation against attacks from enemies who wanted to do his people harm. David was also a masculine presence when he played his anointed music for King Saul and when he wrote the beautiful and poetic Psalms.

How about when he danced so feverishly that his clothes fell off? Yes, masculine.

David was a unique representation of the glory of God in masculine form. However, the enemy hated David's masculine presence, and he assaulted every aspect of David's life where that masculine presence was making a difference.

First, David lost his job. As a result of Saul's jealous rages, David was unable to play his music and sing. He was unable to be the leader of his army. He was unable to be the head of Saul's bodyguards. His presence was no longer wanted. In fact, his presence was marked for an early departure from planet earth.

Assaulted presence. Lost confidence. Escape to the cave and regroup.

The enemy hates a true, God-given masculine presence, because it brings order, safety, security, peace, and harmony.

Remember that we're not talking about some stereotype of masculinity. Outwardly, if this masculine presence looks like anything, it will be different in each of us because each man is unique. Some guys like to play sports and some like to paint. Some men like to hunt and fish and some like to go to the opera. Some like classical music and some like country. Some like barbecue and some sushi. Some like to run marathons and some like to watch all-day movie marathons. Some like suits and ties and some like blue jeans. I was in New York a couple of years ago and saw a guy with a suit coat and blue jeans with tennis shoes. It actually looked pretty good too.

Each of these preferences is masculine and each of them unique. There are a billion other masculine preferences as well, in a billion more categories. How can all of these be masculine? Because they are preferred by men, possessors of X and Y chromosomes.

God made me unique, yet the same as you and other guys. The X and Y, uniquely displayed yet consistently called and designed to bring safety, covering, and peace, first. Called to be a wall of security for our people, in our unique ways.

Just like Role 1, we'll take a look at the nuts and bolts of how this role gets refreshed, touched, tweaked, and changed in the next chapter. But I must share a great Role 2 story with you right now. It comes to us via a powerful little woman.

The men of Briarglen. The church where I am the lead pastor is located in a transitional area of our city. This is an area where the more affluent to middle-class strata of society meet the less affluent.

A battle of sorts is taking place in this part of the city. Many of the houses are becoming rundown, businesses are leaving, and several government-subsidized apartment complexes are within walking distance.

Right in the middle of this area is a little school named Briarglen Elementary School. The principal, Mrs. Tamra Bird, is a little woman with a huge heart. I found this out when I went to meet her in an effort to see how our church might help her, her staff, and her students.

I scheduled an appointment with Tamra and went to see her with a good friend of mine, Tom O'Malley. Tom has been an administrator in the public schools in our city for more than thirty years; in fact, I had dropped his name to get in Tamra's door.

We had a great conversation, getting to know each other, and then I got to the point. I wanted to know how our church might help her and her school. Without flinching, she shot back at me that her students, teachers, and staff desperately needed to have a masculine presence. I asked her to elaborate.

She said that many of her students came from broken homes or homes where there was not a man in the house on a regular basis or maybe at all. Overall, this led to a lack of masculine presence in the students' lives. Tamra then went on to say that she would like for us to have men stand in the cafeteria as her students ate lunch. They would be a presence there, just being men. She wanted these men to talk with the students, learn their names, and just be there. She had no doubt that this would be a comforting presence. What a simple yet profound request.

Tamra really gets it! She understands Role 2 better than many men do—better than I did. She knows that men can bring a unique presence that causes people to feel safe, protected, and provided for.

In response to her request, men from our church have been going to stand at Briarglen for about a year now, and it has been amazing for all of them. It has affirmed to these men that they can simply offer the gift of their masculinity to those in the community who need it.

Several of the men have told me that this simple activity has done more for them than it has for the students. The men realize that it feels good just to be a man. And they gain a greater understanding of what it means to operate in their role as a man, especially Role 2.

In an era when a strong masculine presence is rarely taught or celebrated, Tamra and the men of Briarglen are certainly flowing against the cultural norm. Tamra and her staff report that the school has fewer disciplinary issues and that a calming presence has come into the cafeteria that wasn't there before. Because of this relationship with Briarglen, we've also been able to provide help to several families in crisis.

Being men. Being a presence—a masculine presence that causes those around us to see God in manly fashion and to feel safe.

Role 2 and you. I wonder if David felt his masculine presence being assaulted at first. Maybe not. But eventually he caught on. Every aspect of his presence and his ability to be a man for God had been assaulted. His job: gone. His wife: gone. His best friend: gone. David had no one to be a masculine presence for. Then eventually it occurred to him: "I'll hide with the One who made me a man and see if He can give me a perspective."

Do you feel as if your masculinity has been assaulted? If you don't, you might be numb to the enemy's attacks that prevent you from being a masculine presence for the people in your world.

Maybe you don't feel that you can be the unique man God has created you to be. You feel as if you have to be like every other guy around you—some cookie-cutter version of godly manhood. Well, you don't. There's no life in that.

God desires to affirm you and use you in the unique presentation of the X and Y chromosomes that you are. But to know exactly where and how to be the presence He wants you to be, you must get to the cave. Take your assaulted self and run to the cave. Let God help you, coach you, and release you.

I know that you might be saying, "Would you help me already? Give me some pointers on how to take on the masculine roles that we're talking about." My answer is, "Good! You're seeing the importance of getting to the cave first instead of eventually. You are understanding the significance of hiding in the cave. You're grasping the value of getting your masculine presence recharged and restored!"

So hang on just a bit longer. Let's take a look at how the enemy assaulted just one more role in David's life and how he might do the same in yours.

Assault on Role 3

The final role assaulted in David's life was Role 3: the power to pursue relationships that help men to live well. In its fullest expression, this role is about the power of God revealed between people.

Remember? We concluded that the image of God is expressed on the earth through relationships.

God didn't create men to be by themselves all of the time. We were created to be in relationships. In fact, we *need* relationships in order to survive and to thrive. For a married man, this can happen powerfully with his wife. When a man and a woman are in a healthy marriage relationship, the fullness of God radiates from them. So it makes sense that the enemy will fight feverishly to break up marriages by any means necessary.

This is exactly what happened between David and his wife. As a result of the assaults waged against David, their marriage was attacked. They were separated from each other, and Michal was eventually given to another man:

> But Saul had given his daughter Michal, David's wife, to
> Paltiel son of Laish, who was from Gallim (1 Samuel 25:44).

When he became king, David eventually reclaimed his wife. Yet the breach caused by the earlier assaults upon David's life seemed to prevent him from ever having a child with Michal. Scripture presents a sad ending to their story:

> Michal daughter of Saul had no children to the day of her
> death (2 Samuel 6:23).

Satan knows the potential that resides in a healthy marriage. A healthy marriage will help you live well. In case you think I'm just making a vague statement, consider this: Research done at the University of Colorado examined more than 36,000 adults between the ages of twenty-five and sixty-four. The goal of the study was to look for a connection between marital status and well-being. Here's what the researchers concluded:

> Marriage is believed to protect individuals by focusing on
> health, reducing risks, and increasing compliance with medical

regimens. Those who are not married have higher rates of mortality due to drinking, smoking, risk-taking behaviors, accidents, and chronic disease that require regulated behavior or treatment. Generally, compared with those who are not married, married individuals eat better, take better care of themselves, and live a more stable, secure, and scheduled lifestyle.[21]

Other relationships are vital too. You might not be married yet— or you might never be—but that doesn't mean that you can't have a deep friendship, and it doesn't mean you can't be complete. You most certainly can. David, in the lament he sang upon hearing of Jonathan's death, says that their love for each other was greater than what he had with women:

> Jonathan lies slain on your high places. I am distressed for you, my brother Jonathan; very pleasant have you been to me; your love to me was extraordinary, surpassing the love of women (2 Samuel 1:25-26, NKJV).

This is a powerful statement about what can happen among a band of brothers. We can't read very far into the account of David's life and not be impressed by his friendship with Jonathan. The story of their brotherhood in 1 Samuel 19–20 is really the account of an epic friendship. Their friendship was characterized by a deep love and respect that would see each one defer to the other as it pertained to ascending to the throne. They were also willing to put their lives on the line for each other.

Jonathan had been in the army of Israel and had likely watched David defeat Goliath. He must have been impressed and realized that he would one day meet the legendary young slingshot prodigy who eventually also became his brother-in-law.

Jonathan had every right to be jealous of David, because Jonathan should have been next in line to the throne. However, he wanted God's will more than his own. He did everything necessary to help his friend

David step into God's plan for his life. Jonathan was a friend who helped David to live well.

As men, we need these types of friends. This is the type of brother that a man needs in his band of brothers—a friend who holds his brother accountable, challenging him to change directions if he is headed toward the wrong cave.

Jonathan did all of these things for David, so it would make sense that the enemy would try and steal this relationship from him. Satan will try to steal these types of relationships from you as well. In the next chapter, I'll give you some ideas about how and where to find these types of brothers. But for now, keep in mind that the enemy attacks this role relentlessly. He did it to David and the 400, and he will do it to you as well.

When Role 3 was assaulted in David's life, he needed to go to the cave. While David probably thought he had no friends at all, he had one in God and 400 other friends were on their way as well. David needed the kind of friend described in Proverbs 18:24, which was written by one of David's sons, King Solomon:

> One who has unreliable friends soon comes to ruin, but there
> is a friend who sticks closer than a brother.

The men who joined David in the cave wanted the same things he wanted. They wanted to hear from someone whom they could trust. They desired to be with someone they could depend on at all times. The cave is a place where men find the One who sticks closer than a brother and become like Him for each other.

God brought David 400 brothers. Most of them probably came from the 1,000 men who were under his command. Upon entering the cave, these men were a messed-up group of rebels and hellions. However, something happened in the cave that changed them, and their exploits would eventually become legendary.

They grew to love each other deeply. They loved David so deeply that they would risk their lives to get him a drink of water. They ushered in his reign and helped establish God's nation again. No wonder the enemy fought against their brotherhood.

Role 3 is about pursuing relationships that are designed to help you live well. A wife and a band of brothers. The enemy will assault each one.

Keep in mind that he can do this subtly. No time. Too busy. I can do it all by myself. I can't trust anyone.

Those thoughts are thunder and lightning. Run for the cover of the cave and pursue Role 3.

Lori and a Band of Old Brothers

I remember when I had no band of brothers—no real community to help me pursue living well. Interestingly, I realized that I was missing these relationships right after my emergency room trip, when I was being assaulted on every front in my life. I wasn't meeting with a friend or a group of men that gave me permission to be open and transparent.

Lori, for better or worse. I did have a wife who was doing her best. God taught me community and the power of relationship through her first. She helped me get well and made me want to live well too.

Although Lori was an absolute angel during this time, she didn't totally understand what was going on in my life. I tried to explain the sinking feeling in my stomach and the helplessness I felt. But she wasn't a guy, so she had no frame of reference.

Still, she prayed for me feverishly. I would find little prayer cards under my pillow, where she had written prayers to God on my behalf. I would also find Bible verses written on recipe cards and placed under our mattress. Lori was doing all that she knew how to cover me and help me get better. In a practical way, she also held down many more of the responsibilities in our home than she usually did—and her regular load was a lot. She required very little of me as I tried to get my bearings again. For better or for worse. This had to feel like worse.

Lori even covered for me in relation to my duties at work and helped me start living a new life. Slowly. Step by step. She was there as God called me to the cave and began to work on me there. Both God and Lori were leading me to a place where I could live a transparent life. They encouraged me not to compete and try to prove I was the best. No more performance.

Lori also helped me understand what it meant to receive grace from God, her, and others. I didn't have to prove myself to her. She also held me accountable to start giving grace to others and not expect them to perform in order for me to love them. I would say that she is gifted at holding me accountable in grace.

I love Lori deeply for being the one who walked with me those first days, weeks, and months as I stumbled to the cave. Yet, as great of a job as she did helping me to walk out of the ER and the dark night, Lori is not a man and she couldn't understand what it is to be one. She had no frame of reference.

The band of brothers. At this time, three friends became the first in my band of brothers. Kym Barger was the very first. We had been working at the same church but initially didn't know each other all that well. But when Kym and his wife Kim (funny, isn't it?) attended a Sunday school class that Lori and I taught, we became friends as couples.

This is when I began to go through my dark night of the soul. Although I didn't know it, Barger was dealing with some of the same stuff. Performance, anxiety, panic, and his own little pack of problems. Thunder clouds in our lives.

If you were to ask us who asked the other first, we probably wouldn't be able to tell you. But one day we agreed that we would start meeting to pray or read the Bible, be the head of our houses (whatever that meant), or just try and do something spiritual. We knew that we needed something more than what was going on in our lives—and my visit to the ER during this time helped me to be sure of it.

On the agreed-upon day, we showed up very early in the morning. I wasn't sleeping well anyway, and I'd read that this is how Jesus did it in Mark 1:35: "Very early in the morning, Jesus got up, left the house and went off to a solitary place to pray."

So that's what we did. We sat with each other, early in the morning, in a little upstairs office at my house. This room came to be known as the cave.

There was really no curriculum in the cave, except that we were brutally honest about what we were going through in our lives. We also agreed that we would not tell anyone what the other man had shared. "What was said in the cave stayed in the cave." Brutally honest and doggedly confidential. If you weren't able to handle these rules, you got uninvited. As the group grew, some guys got uninvited.

During several of my sleepless nights, I had stumbled across the narrative of David and his Mighty Men. I felt that we were kind of like them. Assaulted on all fronts and running, we weren't sure of what was going to happen with our lives.

Needing to hide. Running to a cave. Barger and I began to talk about these guys and their journey. How was it like ours? How was it not? What was it like to run and hide in a cave? We even kept it pretty dark in our "cave." For light we lit a candle and called it an indoor campfire. Some of us started bringing little flashlights so that we could see to read—the same kind of lights we would clip onto our hats when we went duck hunting or backpacking. It kind of created a sense of adventure.

This really threw off some guys, especially when they came prepared for a Bible study and it was too dark to read.

It was actually pretty funny.

Little did we know that we were practicing some spiritual disciplines. In the next chapter, we'll unpack this process and the exact disciplines that brought about the change in our lives. But at the top of the list, we were interacting with the Bible and not just reading it. It was becoming life to us, alive in us.

We began to call this time CaveTime and eventually started doing it weekly. We also did it individually at our own homes.

"See you in the cave," we'd say when we saw each other at church. "Cave this week?" we would ask.

It was kind of like our own little movement. Word got out and guys started to hear about this CaveTime thing. Maybe that's how it happened with the 400 that heard about David's cave.

Eventually Barger and I invited other guys to come to our cave. Two of the most consistent were Kent Helms (a.k.a. "Helmsy") and Kenn Love (a.k.a. "Dr. Love"). Kenn had gone to church with Barger and me; he and his wife, Colleen, were in our Sunday school class as well. Kent Helms is someone I met as a result of our sons playing on the same Peewee football team. Barger and I felt like we could trust both of these guys.

I knew there were things that I saw in these guys' character that I admired and needed. Kenn was brutally honest, a faithful follower of Jesus, and a loyal friend. He has proven this to me over and over again. This would be exemplified as he stood by Colleen in her victorious battle with cancer—a battle we fought with him in the cave and one that became ours as well.

I liked Kent Helms the first time I spoke with him on the sidelines of our sons' football game. I liked the way he approached life—honest and straightforward. If Helms tells you he is going to do something, it is money in the bank. And he has one of the best lines about confidentiality that I've ever heard. It came out one day when he was describing how he felt about one of his old friends: "That guy knows where all of the dead bodies are buried in my life." That statement hit me like a ton of bricks. It meant this friend knew some stuff about Kent that Kent wasn't proud of, but his friend would never tell.

CaveTime is about guys with whom you share your stuff—the dead bodies and all—and not get judged or ratted out. I love Helmsy and Dr. Love.

By the way, you might wonder why I titled this section "Lori and a Band of Old Brothers." When Barger, Dr. Love, Helmsy, and I started having CaveTime, we were still relatively young men in our 30s. We've been having CaveTime together in some form or fashion for almost fifteen years, and we're now flirting with the concept of being "old guys."

CaveTime and the band of brothers in the cave have been constants for us. Our time in the cave has helped us to live well, and we are better men for it. We all came to the cave assaulted and struggling, but we've learned how to struggle well, together, in the cave. We have been changed there. Assaulted and then changed.

You were there through the fire, You were there through it all
Never leaving or forsaking, You were there through it all
Brought me out of the ashes, brought me out to become
A mighty wall for Your people, may Your love make us one.

"The Wall" by David Gungor and John Arndt
From *CaveTime: The Escape, A Worship Experience*

I've got 'em right where I want 'em: surrounded from the inside.

—Sergeant First Class Jerry "Mad Dog" Shriver

Chapter 5

BOOT CAMP: *A NEW START*

In the summer of 2011, my oldest son Jacob enlisted in the United States Marine Corps, forever changing him for the better. Jacob joined the Marines because he felt confused about the direction of his life. He told me that he "needed a change," "a fresh start," "some discipline."

While we certainly had discipline at our house when Jacob was growing up, I knew what he meant. And the men Jacob would spend thirteen weeks with in the cave—I mean barracks—were experts at meting it out. They thrived on discipline and focus that would bring about a complete change in his life.

Jacob would be a changed man.

The men who joined David at the cave were confused and looking for a fresh start when they first arrived. The following is novelist Cliff Graham's version of what he thinks might have happened in the cave between 1 Samuel 22:1 and 1 Samuel 25:15-16.

> There are flames. He is testing us, those of us who came to him in the cave. Only the strongest can join him. The ground is on fire all around me. He is testing us, testing us. But we can do this. Run faster now! The log on the rope swings again, almost hits me; I need to keep moving. Faster he shouts, his sword cutting the ropes, sending more logs towards us. Will this never end? Will he never let us rest? But I will not quit. More logs swing toward us. I can

do this. Keep moving faster…"Praise to our God!" David
shouts. "Arrows to our enemies!" We shout back. I feel a hand
on my back. "Well done, man from the south," says the voice
of David. "You have a home among us, if you wish." He is
smiling at me. So are his men. We can join them. A new life
for us. A new start.[22]

In the cave, these 400 distressed, indebted, and discontented men
found a primitive boot camp that would prepare them for some military exploits both miraculous and legendary (see 2 Samuel 23:8-39).
First Samuel 26:15-16 describes the effects of the time that these men
spent in the cave. Their CaveTime produced a major change in them.

> These men were very good to us. They did not mistreat us, and
> the whole time we were out in the fields near them nothing was
> missing. Night and day *they were a wall around us* the whole
> time we were herding our sheep near them (emphasis added).

Wow! Are these the same men? Men who are treating the people
around them well, not plundering or stealing, and even providing
protection? What a powerful characterization about a group of men who
had previously been described as discontented, in debt, and distressed.
What a change.

Until last summer when Jacob entered boot camp, I had no frame of
reference for what might have happened in the cave to change these men
as they traveled the path to become David's Mighty Men. I do now.

Grace

Everyone who enters USMC boot camp is viewed with the same
set of eyes—the eyes of grace. While this might sound strange for the
military, let me explain.

Several days before Jacob left for boot camp, we sat in my office and
talked with a friend of mine, Ed Wright. Ed is a real hero. He was a
Marine, then trained with the Navy SEALs, and eventually became a

Navy pilot. As we talked, Jacob shared a bit with Ed about his story. College hadn't worked out for him, nor had almost anything else he'd tried. Jacob was dealing with some pretty significant feelings of guilt, shame, and failure. What would they think of him? Would he measure up? Would he make it? How did he know that he wouldn't fail at this too? Can you say thunderclouds? Assault?

Upon hearing Jacob express his feelings, Ed leaned forward, looked Jacob in the eyes—right through to his spine—and said, "Jacob, when you go to the Corps, none of that matters. When you put your feet on the yellow footprints on the walkway in front of those doors at the training depot and walk through those doors, none of that matters."

With growing passion in his voice, Ed continued: "In the eyes of the Corps, your life starts from that day forward. Your past doesn't matter. Those guys are your brothers, and they won't let you fail. It's not an option."

Then Ed looked even deeper into Jacob's eyes, right down to his soul, and said, "I am your brother. Semper fi. Oorah."

I wanted to cry, shout, salute, sing the national anthem and the "Battle Hymn of the Republic," then go and tell my wife that I was going to enlist. I wanted to be Ed's brother, too. Jacob's brother. Lori said that I couldn't sign up.

Probably without realizing it, Ed had described grace. A fresh start for a confused young man. No turning back. No focus on the past. It was as if his sins would be thrown as far as the east is from the west. A young man who had weathered some assaults and some confusion was ready to walk through those doors Ed spoke of and get rid of the baggage—the mental assaults that haunted him.

I think that the 400 must have felt much the same. They left behind whatever life they had. They had arrived at the cave, assaulted in their masculinity. Their roles had been confused, blurred, and battered, and their CaveTime would provide clarity and definition. They would have no doubt about what their roles were.

The same was true for Jacob. No doubt. He would know exactly where he was going to fit in this wall of changed men.

You can change, too. You are never too far gone. When you decide to enter the cave, those shameful, haunting thoughts and actions—your sins—are dealt with. They don't preclude you from going in. God whispers that you are welcome in the cave. But you must be ready to submit to the process in order to be changed.

The Process Begins: Get Some Stones

In order for Jacob to change, he knew he needed some weaponry that he didn't already possess. Primarily, these were the weapons of discipline and focus. To kill the giants that were assaulting him, he needed some unconventional weapons.

The 400 also knew they needed some help as well. While we can't be sure if the giants assaulting those men were exactly like the one that David had killed (although Goliath might have had four brothers), they were still very intimidating. As we discussed in Chapter 2, debt can be daunting. Distress can be debilitating. Despondency can leave you with no hope. These are giants. Those men faced them, and we do as well. They are relentless.

The 400 knew that David had killed a giant. They knew that this fierce warrior was their best bet to survive the assaults being waged against them. Because he had faced Goliath, maybe he could help them face their assaults. Maybe they could find out his secret and learn to fight as he did. Something about David was oddly different from other warriors they'd seen or fought with, and they wanted some of what he had. They were adept at spear throwing, sword fighting, and clubbing opponents to death, but maybe he would teach them how to use stones as proficiently as he did:

> Then he [David] took his staff in his hand, *chose five smooth stones* from the stream, put them in the pouch of his shepherd's

bag and, with his sling in his hand, approached the Philistine (1 Samuel 17:40).

In order to face the giant Goliath, David used a weapon he was already proficient with—a sling with a stone in it. While this choice certainly seems unconventional, he had practiced with this weapon over and over again. Further, he was confident about what God would do through him on that day. He was also aware that he needed to fight, yet fighting didn't seem to intimidate him. A giant was still just a target—albeit a bigger and slower one.

> As the Philistine moved closer to attack him, David ran quickly toward the battle line to meet him. Reaching into his bag and taking out a stone, he slung it and struck the Philistine on the forehead. The stone sank into his forehead, and he fell face down on the ground (1 Samuel 17:48-49).

David certainly wasn't afraid—he ran right toward his foe!

You might wonder, *If he was so confident, then why did he choose five stones?* I don't believe he thought it would really take five shots to kill that huge target. My guess is that he chose five stones to kill Goliath's four brothers, who eventually died at the hands of his army in a later battle anyway:

> In still another battle, which took place at Gath, there was a huge man with six fingers on each hand and six toes on each foot—twenty-four in all. He also was descended from Rapha. When he taunted Israel, Jonathan son of Shimeah, David's brother, killed him. These four were descendants of Rapha in Gath, and they fell at the hands of David and his men (2 Samuel 20:20-22).

Regardless of his reasons for the choosing of five stones, David was prepared for anything and anyone he found himself up against. I believe this attitude drew the 400 men to David in the cave. They needed some confidence, and that was his game.

In the same way, Jacob needed some discipline and direction, and that was the Marines' game. They have been doing it for more than 230 years. They do it so well that the USMC is considered the world's most elite fighting force. To be part of that force would give any man confidence.

To be part of David's force would make any man mighty.

Little did the men in the cave with David know that they would not be trained merely in the art of physical warfare. They also would engage in spiritual and emotional warfare. While they would be escaping physical enemies, they would also learn to face the spiritual and emotional giants that accompany the physical ones. I am talking about the kinds of giants that haunt you when you deal with the debts, distress, and despondency these men did.

Giants like to inflict shame, pain, terror, fear, relational trauma, panic, addictions, value by performance, abuse, and the list goes on. These men would learn to face and slay their intimidators with both physical and spiritual stones. Yes, David taught them how to use physical stones to be placed in slings and hurled at huge targets. But perhaps more importantly, he taught them how to identify, hone, and use their spiritual stones to hurl at targets that aren't always so easy to see.

Mighty-Men-in-the-making must learn to use their stones.

A Smelly Reunion

I'm not sure how these men knew to find David in the cave. But word must have traveled quickly in outlaw circles, because these 400 showed up. I can't help but think that the entrance of the first man into the cave, following David, went something like this:

> He heard a rustling in the bushes outside of the entrance to the cave. "David?" the voice half whispered. No response. "David? Are you there?" Still no response. David heard feet sliding around in the dirt at the mouth of the cave, then tripping over a log he had placed there. The voice, now closer and not

whispering quite as softly this time, said, "David, I know that you're here. I can feel you. I can smell you. We have fought together too many times for me to not recognize that odor. You have a distinct smell when you sweat. I smell that smell. It is the smell of sweat, blood, dirty feet, and yes, sheep dung. Yes, isn't that smell that I smell that of my sheepherder king? Do I smell in this cave the smell of my favorite sheepherder king with sheep dip on his sandals?" he spoke tauntingly.

David recognized this voice. It was Josheb-Basshebeth, one of the fiercest warriors David had ever known. Next to Jonathan, this man was one of David's closest friends and comrades. Or so he thought. Was Josheb helping Saul? Had he become a bounty hunter? Surely not him. Sheep dip? Favorite sheepherder king? David actually fought back a little snicker. He hadn't snickered in a long time. It felt good. He loved Josheb deeply because their bond had been forged in brutal life-and-death combat.

Josheb loved David too, and he absolutely loved to tease David about his shepherding days. He told him regularly that he smelled like sheep dung. When he was around David, Josheb would even look at the bottom of David's sandals as if he were checking for sheep dung.

How funny.

Right now, though, David was a little too embarrassed to show himself to his friend. You'll recall that he had spit on his own face and had used the bathroom on himself for good measure to ensure that the boys back in Gath believed he truly was crazy. That was another in the combination of smells that Josheb was picking up on. David needed to put on a fresh set of clothes.

"I heard what happened in Gath," Josheb declared, "and I know that you were faking it. You aren't crazy. I believe in you. You are my king, even if I can't see you. I can smell you, though, my king. Come on David. Show yourself, my friend. I know that you're in there. Don't spear me, I'm coming in deeper. When I said that I would follow you anywhere, I meant it. I will die with you. I will die for you, David. You are still God's anointed, and He sent me to tell you that. I have no life if it is not spent fighting the battles of our LORD, together, you and I, side by side."

David saw Josheb holding a torch, intently looking for any sign of life. David could tell by looking at his eyes that Josheb was there out of concern. Ever so slowly, David moved toward the light of the torch. Quietly, tentatively, like a dog with his tail between his legs, he dragged himself into the light and said to his friend, "Sheepherder king? Does it really smell that horrible in here?"

Finally, the two embraced like long-lost brothers. Their reunion was cut short, however, as they heard the distinct sounds of men in flight. Swords clanging and canteens sloshing—more men were definitely scurrying and scrambling up the narrow path on the hillside, as if they were trying to escape from something, too.

I imagine more and more men came to the cave on a daily basis. One day there were two. Then came ten. On another day there were six and then maybe twenty, until eventually, 400 came to find David and submit to him as their leader and king.

I believe that God sent each of these men to David there in the cave for at least four reasons:

1. God would do something in each of these men's lives to restore them individually and wanted to meet with them about it. (Remember Role 1?)

2. God would give them some stones and deliver them from their debts, distresses, and discontentments, so that they might function as a healthy masculine presence in their world (Role 2).

3. God would provide a community of healthy men so that He might use them as an army (Role 3).

4. God wanted to remind David that he wasn't forgotten. God indeed had a plan! While it looked different than David expected, its implementation was right on schedule.

In healthy relationships with others, men experience a unique and masculine type of fulfillment—one filled with camaraderie, accountability, challenge, and instruction about how to walk in their masculine roles. David had this with Jonathan before his friend was taken away, and he would most definitely have some close relationships with the men who sought him out in the cave. These relationships, forged in the fires of escape, conflict, and struggle for survival, gave birth to some amazingly deep and masculine bonds that would change the history of their nation, and even the history of the world.

The stone of community is powerful, providing an amazing synergy that occurs as men begin to walk in their masculinity and join with others who know what that means as well. They become a powerful unit.

In the next five chapters, we'll take a look at what I believe are the five spiritual stones used by David and the 400 in their journey to becoming the Mighty Men. As we focus on these weapons and how to use them in our own lives, I believe you will learn to face the giants assaulting you.

As you witness the change that occurred in the lives of David and his men and those in our day who have learned to use these weapons, you'll decide to show up and become a changed man too.

I am like an olive tree
flourishing in the house of God;
I trust in God's unfailing love
for ever and ever.
For what you have done I will always praise you
in the presence of your faithful people.
And I will hope in your name,
for your name is good.

—Psalm 52:8-9

The here-and-now is no mere filling of time, but a
filling of time with God.

—John W. Foster

Chapter 6

STONE 1: *SHOW UP*

I always remember the day that my wife and I took Jacob to the shipping station as he left for boot camp. That's the day his life changed. It was simple: Jacob showed up.

When it comes to the cave, that's what each of us must decide to do as well. We must be intentional to show up.

I am an early morning guy, so I set my alarm for a time in the early morning to help me show up for my individual CaveTime. Some guys show up to meet with God during the lunch hour. Some while working out. Some in the evening. The point is this: If you're going to become a changed man, you need to make a decision to show up at a certain time and at a particular place in order to leave the assaults and pressures behind.

Show up and get to the cave. God is waiting there to help, but you must decide to go and get the help. That's exactly what David did:

> David left Gath and escaped to the cave of Adullam (1 Samuel 22:1).

David and the 400 had to show up to the cave in order to eventually become a legendary fighting force. They each had different reasons for being there, but they all knew they needed something. They all wanted to escape the assaults.

They also needed answers to questions about their roles and direction about how to operate within their roles. They had to get training, gain focus, and define their mission. But before they could even work on attaining these desired goals, they first had to show up.

Remember Role 1? You were created to be with God first—to have an individual relationship with Him, and to show up on behalf of those who look to you for covering and care, before anyone else does. This is the foundation that CaveTime is built upon. Showing up starts the process and affirms you in your first role.

When

When does the process start for a recruit in the Marines? For Jacob, it began the moment he walked through the doors of the Recruit Training Depot. While the Marines extend grace, it's their own unique brand of grace! The recruit is stripped of everything that defines him as an individual. His clothes and personal belongings are taken, and his head is shaved. He is made to look like everyone else, and he gets a bunk, (rack) in the barracks. This will be his cave for the next three months.

Jacob told me that immediately he felt that it was not about him or anything he had done in the past. It's not about old associations or mistakes. It's not about all of the great things that he's done or how well he performed.

Like my friend Ed said to Jacob that day in my office, "The slate has been wiped clean. You'll have a fresh start."

In Philippians 3:12-14, the apostle Paul describes this grace-filled process that starts with just showing up:

> Not that I have already obtained all this, or have already arrived at my goal, but I press on to take hold of that for which Christ Jesus took hold of me. Brothers and sisters, I do not consider myself yet to have taken hold of it. But one thing I do: Forgetting what is behind and straining toward what is ahead, I press on toward the goal to win the prize for which God has called me heavenward in Christ Jesus.

Paul was a caveman, wasn't he? Just as the Marine recruit has a clean slate when he shows up to boot camp, you have a clean slate with God when you show up in the cave. You need to know immediately that you aren't judged for anything.

The 400 weren't judged. They were allowed in, in spite of their debt, distress, and discontentment. They showed up to be with David. Jacob showed up at the Training Depot to meet with the drill instructor and move forward with his training. And you and I need to make an appointment to show up to be with Jesus and press on with our training. He reminds you to forget the past intimidations, mistakes, and failures, and instead to look ahead.

For the Marine recruit, the legendary drill instructor is the man who will lead him in the change process. According to Jacob, as the DI helps and instructs the recruit 24/7, he definitely helps a man forget the old ways and patterns.

When we enter the cave, this is what I call the individual aspect of change. Each of us must go to the cave to be changed individually. We must go by ourselves. A man and his God. Alone. Once again, the apostle Paul nails it:

> I have been crucified with Christ and I no longer live, but Christ lives in me. The life I now live in the body, I live by faith in the Son of God, who loved me and gave himself for me (Galatians 2:20).

Notice the personal pronoun "I"? Paul says that to show up is a decision a man must make for himself. I need to choose to show up to the cave and be with Jesus. There, I can meet with Him and exercise my faith in His ability to lead me forward.

CaveTime also has a team aspect. But it's imperative to understand that you must show up yourself. You must do what it takes to get to the cave and spend some time with Jesus. Only then can He direct you and begin to change you.

Where

The Marines have their barracks. David and the 400 had their cave at Adullam. So where do we regular X and Y guys show up?

This question has many answers. As I said, I'm an early morning person, so I set my alarm for a time long before the sun comes up and head to my cave after getting a cup of morning brew. I had one guy ask me if my cave was a real rock one—with a campfire, dirt, and all of the cave trimmings. Regrettably, I had to tell him no. But mine is still pretty cool. It's a room at the back of my house that was built on an old patio slab.

This "cave" is particularly great for groups of men. It has great access from the outside, so guys who join me during the week don't have to walk through my house. Despite no dirt floors and fire pit (although both would be very cool), I do have the room decorated the way I want it. Pictures of John Wayne hang on the walls. Lighting comes from a chandelier made of antlers. Duck decoys line the windows. On the walls are stuffed ducks and a huge trout that my wife's grandpa caught. A fake wood-burning stove/heater has a light that looks like glowing wood.

I'll admit that just describing my cave with its outdoorsy stuff makes me feel good. But that's just me. Whatever works for you and your situation is great. Some guys have their caves in the car on the way to work. I know one guy used his car as his cave just so he could have some privacy. You might find a nearby coffee shop that you head to each morning for CaveTime. Other men have personal CaveTime when they're running, walking, riding a horse, or walking the dog.

The point is that you need to show up and be with Jesus first. You and Him. The two of you.

When you do this consistently, you will be changing. It's inevitable.

All I Could Do

I began to understand the power of the message of just showing up when a friend told me about his experience with this stone.

Cal had just gone through a horrible divorce. His ex-wife had been both physically and emotionally abusive to him. She had committed adultery numerous times and had also run up staggering debt on their credit cards. This guy had all of the three Ds happening in his life at once, and he was barely functioning.

Going to work was a major challenge for Cal. He hadn't gone to church in months, but a friend invited him to a CaveTime at his house. Cal dug in his heels and said there was no way he was going to another lame Bible study and feel shamed and unworthy while being stared at.

Cal's friend convinced him that CaveTime wasn't that way and asked him to try it once. To get him off his back, Cal gave in and said okay. As he approached his friend's house and entered the study, there were no lights on—just a candle.

"Pretty weird," Cal mumbled under his breath. But he felt his way across the floor with his foot, kind of like a blind man using a cane, and he stumbled into a chair. None of the other guys came that day, so the two of them just sat there. Cal said he felt like trash, and the weight and shame he felt were almost unbearable.

He actually fell to his knees and got on his face. The sun was starting to come up, and as a bit of light shone in the window, his buddy just began to pray for him, over him, placing a hand on his shoulder. There was no Bible reading that day. No questions asked. Just two guys showing up to the cave.

Cal said this process went on for about a year. All he could do was show up and be there. Eventually, he began showing up in his own cave too, as he learned from his faithful friend. He told me that showing up saved his life. It might save yours too.

To Be with Dad

One of the most gratifying feelings imaginable is when I get a message from someone that expresses sentiments like the ones in the note below from my friend Jerry.

I was Jerry's youth pastor when he was a confused junior high student. I remember picking him up from school and going to Taco Bell for lunch. Man could that kid eat tacos! We'd talk and laugh. He was starved for appropriate male affection, and I gave him what I could. He desperately wanted a father. I spent time with him, but I had a growing family of my own.

When we eventually moved away, Jerry was hurt, feeling abandoned by yet another father figure. More than anything, he needed to be loved and affirmed by his heavenly Father. I'll let him tell you in his own words about the power of just showing up to be with God:

> As a young man who lost his father to suicide when I was a teenager, I have struggled my entire life, making many mistakes trying to figure out what it means to be a man. Even more complex has been the conceptualization process of what it means to be in a relationship with God. CaveTime has provided me the invaluable gift of a biblically based method of how to engage in my relationship with Jesus. CaveTime is Dad time for me; it provides me the tools needed to establish a habit of seeking healthy relationship with our Lord and Savior. This time with my Father is my place of refuge, and I know the continued practice of going into the cave will only strengthen my spirit, heart, and mind. This gives me the ability to be the *real* man of God I am called to be. CaveTime teaches me to be a man of action, one who engages in real conversation with God, and that is what it is to be a real man, one who leans solely on Christ.
>
> —JERRY DARNELL, CAVEMAN

Jerry is now in graduate school, training to be a counselor. What an amazing story!

When Jerry says that showing up to be with God is his Dad time, he means it. Just Jerry and his Dad, together in the cave. This sets the stage for conversations and instruction that no one else can give him. I love Jerry like a son, but I can't give him what his heavenly Father and Creator can when they both show up for CaveTime.

Not Afraid of the Dark

When I first started having a personal CaveTime, I actually did it in the dark. Sound strange? Part of the reason involves where I was emotionally after my ER experience and my conversation with the doctor informing me I was having panic attacks.

When I returned from my hospital visit, I continued to have trouble sleeping. I seemed to be up at all hours of the night. We had four young children, so I couldn't just turn on the lights in the house. So I decided to start just sitting with Jesus, focusing on the fact that He was there with me.

I was not alone. I felt assaulted and tired. But I made a decision to invite Him into my sleeplessness. I didn't read the Bible, although at times I recited Scripture by memory. But the focus was on *being*, not on *doing*.

I was showing up to be with Jesus.

I didn't even know it at the time, but I was actually coming into the cave for the first time. I thought I was inviting God to spend time with me, but I soon realized that He was already at the threshold of the cave, inviting me to come and be with Him.

I was showing up to be with Him. I just sat with Him, sometimes for more than just a few minutes.

Many great men in Scripture showed up to be with their Lord—just the two of them.

Of course, we've looked at David. But he had practiced this even before he escaped to the cave at Adullam, such as when he tended his father's sheep (1 Samuel 16:11). Another was Elijah, who also retreated to a cave when he was assaulted by Jezebel (1 Kings 19).

Jesus spent time with the heavenly Father many times: early in the morning (Mark 1:35), in the mountains (Luke 6:12), in private (Luke 9:18), on a boat (Matthew 14:13), and as He was being assaulted relentlessly in the Garden at Gethsemane (Mark 14:32).

I was following in the footsteps of many other men who had gone before me. I was showing up.

I hope I've shown you how important it is to make a decision to show up. Just like I did in the dark. Just like my friend Jerry did to spend time with his Dad. Just like Cal, who was so broken he could only lay on the floor. All of us showed up.

This is where the process begins, with a decision that regardless of what else is going on in your life, your first priority is to be with Jesus.

Make an appointment to be with Him in the morning, evening, in your car, or on the bus. Show up in the cave to be with The Cave.

Note: I am not leaving you hanging here. You'll find some ideas on making the most of the stone of showing up in "Strap on the Toolbelt: Tools for Practicing the Stones," at the end of this book. If you are struggling to show up and spend time alone with God, I urge you to turn to that section now.

My heart, O God, is steadfast,
my heart is steadfast;
I will sing and make music.
Awake, my soul!
Awake, harp and lyre!
I will awaken the dawn.
I will praise you, LORD, among the nations;
I will sing of you among the peoples.
For great is your love, reaching to the heavens;
your faithfulness reaches to the skies.
Be exalted, O God, above the heavens;
let your glory be over all the earth.

—Psalm 57:7-11

Learn to worship God as the God who does
wonders, who wishes to prove in you that He can
do something supernatural and divine.

—Andrew Murray

Chapter 7

STONE 2: *WORSHIP*

The Marines taught Jacob something about worship, and I learned it as well.

After Jacob showed up and was given grace USMC-style, he was introduced to the power of a man's song. He shared with me that for hours and hours each day, he was given the "opportunity" to march. Jacob said that's how the drill instructors described it. As the recruits marched, they repeated a cadence called out by the DI. The cadence was a song that would help the recruits march at a specific pace to the other side of the parade deck.

The parade deck is a large and hallowed tarmac, the size of several football fields, which only Marines can stand and march on. While some of the cadence songs are legendary for their coarseness, many of them speak of the historic battles and values of the Corps. Watching the Marines march was very moving, and Jacob has expressed to me that it was very powerful to be a part of.

The power of men singing and chanting in unison was awesome for Jacob to experience. And on one particular day it made a lasting impact on my understanding of the power of worship in men's lives as well.

USMC-Style Worship

The day of Jacob's boot camp graduation ceremony is indelibly etched into my memory, and it deeply moved our entire family. The 600 graduating Marines finished marching on the parade deck, with the Marine Corps band playing some of the most amazing marching music I've ever heard. At a particular point in the ceremony, the band stopped. Then the recruits stopped and stood at parade rest. At that point the general greeted and welcomed the graduates' families.

He then asked us if we would excuse him as he greeted his Marines. He spun around, faced the young Marines, and barked out a hearty "Good morning Marines." The crowd was then rocked with emotion, when in unison the young Marines roared back, "Good morning sir, OOOOOOORAAAAAAHHH!!"

The ground shook with their response, and I had never been so proud of my son and my country. Rest assured that if this forty-nine-year-old could have run out onto the parade deck and signed up that day, I would have. Lori had to hold me back, even though my seventy-one-year-old father was practically right behind me! The loud and powerful voices of masculine warriors facing their commander was both awesome and powerful.

I pray that our voices may do the same. OOOOOOraaaah to our God! OOOOOOrraaaaaahhhhh Jesus!

Whether in quiet words during the dark night, loud words at any time of the day, or in unison with some other men who are ready to shake the ground with their mouths in worship of the King, we must worship Him with our mouths. Quiet and with tears. Loud and with spinning and leaping.

Songs from the Cave

I'm sure that David's men also had their chants and cadences. Initially, they probably spoke of David and his skills, recounting the day he cut down Goliath. I imagine they sang of his victories as a military leader and his being anointed as king. Remember, he was a rock star and hit songs had been written about him. The men who came to the cave had confidence in their leader and what God had done through him, and they very likely expressed their loyalty as they prepared for battle. As the men sang their praises to David and he then pointed them to his God, their confidence was built and they were emboldened.

The Psalms are full of songs like these. Many were written during the time in the cave and have been called the Cave Psalms. They include Psalms 18, 52, 55, 57, 59, and 142. I urge you to read them and speak the words to God with your own voice. Pay attention to what it does to the fire level in your heart.

As they sang those songs, David would remind them that God was their true leader. David urged them to turn their faces towards God and worship in faith. I encourage you to do the same thing. Like the 400, your confidence level in God will be built up, and you too will become a wall. Like the 400, Jacob in the Marines, and me in my dark night, your debts, distresses, and despondency will be dealt with by the fiery gaze of a loving God.

The song of those who possess the X and Y, as they escape the assaults and hide in the cave, is a powerful thing. It's a mighty stone. Sing it! Sling the stone of worship.

Dancing and Leaping

The introduction to Psalm 34 provides some great insight about how important worship was in David's life.

> I will extol the LORD at all times; his praise will always be on my lips. I will glory in the LORD; let the afflicted hear and rejoice. Glorify the LORD with me; let us exalt his name together (Psalm 34:1-3).

This man was much more than a recreational worshipper. He did a lot more than just mumble along a little bit to worship at church. David was a man passionate about worship—both alone and in a crowd:

> So it was, when those bearing the ark of the LORD had gone six paces, that he sacrificed oxen and fatted sheep. Then David danced before the LORD with all his might; and David was wearing a linen ephod. So David and all the house of Israel brought up the ark of the LORD with shouting and with the sound of the trumpet. Now as the ark of the LORD came into the City of David, Michal, Saul's daughter, looked through a window and saw King David leaping and whirling before the LORD; and she despised him in her heart (2 Samuel 6:13-16, NKJV).

With his leaping and spinning, David worshipped so feverishly that his wife was apparently more than embarrassed. I'll admit that I've seen that look on my wife's face, too, but it wasn't because I had lost myself in worship. Often, I've gotten that "look" when my clothes didn't match or when I said something she deemed as inappropriate in a public setting.

I love David's fire. God, please give us a fire for worship. Fire us up for worship O Lord!

Worship Alone

I'm convinced that David was also a deep and fiery worshipper even when no one was watching. Again in Psalm 34, notice the personal pronouns and the change from "*I* will extol (bless) the Lord" in verse 1, to "Let *us* exalt His name together" in verse 3:

> I will extol the LORD at all times; his praise will always be on my lips. I will glory in the LORD; let the afflicted hear and rejoice. Glorify the LORD with me; let us exalt his name together (Psalm 34:1-3).

David was comfortable worshipping by himself. While the text doesn't specifically say, I imagine that David worshipped when he tended his father's sheep. I wonder if David even sang to his sheep. Just David, God, and the sheep. He sang in worship to God and the sheep received the benefit as they heard his comforting, soothing voice.

I wonder what would happen if we worshipped in our homes? What would that do for the "sheep" there—our children as they slept or went about their days? For our wives? It didn't matter to David if anyone else was around or even listening to him; he was singing for God and to God.

He loved to sing for his God. He knew the Lord deeply. This type of relationship can only come from showing up and having alone time, one on one in the cave with God.

Song in the Dark Night

I remember when I discovered the power of this second stone. It occurred during the same period of time when I started to understand the power of just showing up, as I spent my time alone with God in the darkness of our home.

While things were slowly getting better for me after the ER, I would still battle feelings of panic and anxiety—those threatening feelings that something bad was going to happen. I still wrestled with the knot in my stomach that came from thinking I just wasn't doing enough to please the people around me—and ultimately, not enough for Jesus either.

I realized that I needed to show up and escape every day. I also discovered that I needed to escape not to prove anything or to compete, but simply to meet with Jesus. And while just being with Him was good, I found myself wanting to say something. It was like a little tiny spark or ember of a fire was burning in me—a desire to verbalize my heart toward Him to tell Him what I felt, how I felt, and how I wanted to feel.

In the late hours of the night and the earliest moments of the morning, I was showing up. One part of a poem written in the 16th century by St. John of the Cross titled "Dark Night of the Soul" describes precisely how I felt at this time in my life:

All in the dark went right,
Down secret steps, disguised in other clothes,
(O coming of delight!)
In dark when no one knows,
When all my house lay long in deep repose.

And in the luck of night
In secret places where no other spied
I went without my sight
Without a light to guide
Except the heart that lit me from inside.[23]

In the dark of the night in my escape, I felt a tugging from God. I realized that the ember inside me needed to be stoked into a fire by showing up to be with Him. I also realized that this was a new fire, not the insatiable fire of performance that could only be fed by competition. Those fires had assaulted me and caused me to burn out and end up in the ER. No, this new fire was different, and it could only be fueled by showing up and expressing my heart toward God.

I found myself wanting to worship—wanting to fill that hole in me with worship to God.

Because it was very early in the morning, Handel's *Messiah* and its *Hallelujah Chorus* weren't options. So I latched onto some worship songs of a more quiet and sedate nature and began to sing along with them. I cried with them. At that stage of my life, I didn't cry much (though that has certainly changed since then). So I knew something was up.

I found that when you're in a dark night period and you need a fire from heaven, you worship differently. Deeper. And with a longing to connect. I needed Jesus to touch my heart. I needed Him to heal me.

I needed Him to fill the hole in me. I began to worship differently. No competition. No trying to get Him to love me more. He already loved me as much as He ever could, and I was beginning to know it and even feel it.

I know that worship was a big part of this new fire. This worship was more than a guy checking the church service worship box off of my "do good this week" list. This was real fire.

I was showing up, worshipping God, and being filled.

Burning away the Shame

The fires of worship that burned throughout David's life were kindled in the cave. They sustained him during his time in the dark and also through many situations later in his life. They will burn for you and me too. If we let Him, God can use these fires to burn away the shame and embarrassment that plague all of us as a result of our many failures. These are giants that intimidate, crazy monarchs that send hit squads, and the thunder and lightning that chase and assault us all.

David gives us one last insight into the necessity of this stone in dealing with the debilitating effects of shame and embarrassment:

> I sought the LORD, and he answered me; he delivered me from all my fears. Those who look to him are radiant; their faces are never covered with shame (Psalm 34:4-5).

There in the cave, with spit on his face, David says in Psalm 34:1, "I will [bless] the Lord at all times; His praise will always be on my lips." This meant that David was there in the dark of the cave, telling God how good and powerful He is. David even thanked God for his situation.

Are you serious? David was running! He was an embarrassment. He looked like a failure. He'd acted shamefully by spitting on his own face. In David's culture, the beard was seen as the expression of a man's honor and masculinity. Spitting on someone's beard was to defile him. To spit on your own beard was insane![24] But David was committed to worship even in the middle of acting like a fool.

That's called faith. It is faith that's expressed even when things don't look good. Faith that believes beyond appearances. Faith that ignites change in a man. Faith that brings about miracles. Faith that will change you and me.

David's faith explains why Goliath fell. It shows why men gathered around him. This faith demonstrates how and why the men became a wall.

Faith-filled worship, during the dark night, in the cave.

I could take a lesson or two from David. Could you? How could he worship with such faith? He knew that when he showed up and turned his face toward God in worship, he would be cleaned up. He knew that God would deal with the spit and the foolishness and the mess. Those circumstances are no match for the gaze of a loving Father as He looks at us, His kids. He burns the mess and foolishness away.

> Those who look to him are *radiant*; their faces are never covered with shame (Psalm 34:5).

In this Psalm, David is referring to the bright light beaming from the face of God, which dissipates and burns off all the nastiness from the face of the individual looking at Him.

Worship is like the turning of your face toward God. While your natural instinct in your shame is to look away and turn your face down, David encourages you to look directly toward God. Show up and look at God through worship.

Now I know what the old hymn I grew up singing called "Turn Your Eyes Upon Jesus" means when it speaks of looking at Jesus' face. If you don't remember it, here are the words:

> *O soul, are you weary and troubled?*
> *No light in the darkness you see?*

There's a light for a look at the Savior,
And life more abundant and free!

Turn your eyes upon Jesus,
Look full in His wonderful face,
And the things of earth will grow strangely dim,
In the light of His glory and grace.[25]

The "things of earth" might be spit stains, shame smudges, and embarrassment bruises that all of us wear. But we can look to God, and He will clean off our faces. Get to the cave and let the fire of His gaze burn away the mess. When men are willing to do this, individually and in groups, a battle cry eventually goes forth. Stones are slung and giants fall.

Your Cave Song

Before we move on to examine the next stone, I want to remind you that Stone 1 is all about showing up. You need to make a daily appointment to show up and be with Jesus because that stone is the foundation that the rest of the CaveTime process is built on.

When will your appointment with God take place? Where will you meet with Him? Will you do it in the morning? Afternoon? Evening? In just showing up, you will set the powerful CaveTime process in motion.

Once you show up in the cave—wherever that might be—you'll instinctively want to verbalize your feelings toward Him. Remember, regardless of what your circumstances look like, you can use the power of Stone 2 to worship God with your mouth. Taking this step ignites your faith and begins to take your attention off of the giants of shame, debt, panic, or whatever else is chasing you. Worship focuses you on the face of Jesus.

One way to do this is to find some type of worship music that helps you sing. I began earlier chapters of this book with some of the words from songs on the *CaveTime: A Worship Experience* CD. You can purchase this CD on iTunes or on the CaveTime.org website. This CD is a tool that can help you become proficient in the use of Stone 2. The five songs, based on David's Cave Psalms, are intended to help you verbalize your feelings toward Jesus. I urge you to learn these songs and turn your eyes toward Him. Remember what David said happens when a man does this? The shame on his face is replaced by God's brightness.

The *CaveTime* CD was designed to help you memorize some worship songs and get them deep in your heart and mind. To help you accomplish this, the CD also includes instrumental versions of the five songs. This allows you to learn the songs and then play the instrumental versions to sing without the vocalists on the CD. I know this will take your worship experience to a deeper level.

Note: Just as with Stone 1, I have also provided some additional ideas on making the most of your worship times. If you need help getting started— or you just have one of those days when you don't feel like spending time in worship—I urge you to go to "Strap on the Toolbelt: Tools for Practicing the Stones," at the end of this book and make use of the additional tools provided there.

I cry aloud to the LORD;
I lift up my voice to the LORD for mercy.
I pour out before him my complaint;
before him I tell my trouble.
When my spirit grows faint within me,
it is you who watch over my way.

—Psalm 142:1-3

When you are in the dark, listen, and God will
give you a very precious message.

—Oswald Chambers

Chapter 8

STONE 3: *PRAYER*

When I was a boy, my father had a job that would sometimes take him out of town for a week at a time. I absolutely hated it when he left. Something just felt unsafe and out of whack when he was gone.

But as much as I hated for him to be gone, I loved Fridays. On Friday, I knew he would show up at our front door, walk in, put down his briefcase and say, "Hey bud, come here. I missed you! Here's a surprise. Let's go play catch after I kiss your mom." I then form tackled him around his knees, he picked me up and kissed me and tickled me, and everything was all better.

Dad was home. It just felt safer with him there.

CaveTime is a lot like this. You show up and God meets you there. Just being in God's presence is like my dad coming home, speaking to me, and making everything all right. Role 1, our individual relationship with God, is strengthened when we show up. As a man, this time with God is what you were made for.

Then, we turn our faces to God in worship. All I had to do was see my dad's face, and I felt safe again. When we worship God, He picks us up, looks at us and our shame, and He enables us to deal with those giants that have been assaulting and chasing.

Daddy's home!

Conversations

And then, much like my dad and I going out to play catch—having that father-son conversation and talking about everything that happened that week—is like us praying to God in our CaveTime. God wants us to just have a talk with Him.

Philosophy professor, speaker, and author Dallas Willard puts it this way:

> The effect of conversing with God cannot help but to have a pervasive and spiritually strengthening effect on *all* aspects of our personality. That conversation, when it is truly a conversation, makes an indelible impression on our minds, and our consciousness of him remains vivid as we go our way.[26]

This is a great description of prayer. Prayer is simply a real conversation with God—just as real as if you were sitting down and speaking with a loving father over a meal or a cup of coffee.

The talks I had with my dad when I was a boy remained in my mind and affected me even when he was away. I'd remember what he had said to me, that he loved me, and his promise to see me soon. These words, spoken in conversations while throwing a ball, would sustain me until he got home again.

Eventually he would come home and we'd speak again. He'd ask what I'd done during the week and if I had fun. Had I been a good boy? I'd tell him, "Yes sir." And I remember that he would always say that he wasn't surprised at all because I had "come from good stock." He always said that with a grin on his face. I'd tell him about football practice, when our next game was, and that the same kid who picked on me was still at it. My dad asked me if I needed help with the kid and I would say, "Naw, I just wanted you to know about it. I'll let you know if I need any help."

Reassurance

I remember a time when it wasn't a kid in my class who was picking on me, but a dad. I was only in sixth grade and had recently asked Jesus into my heart. This guy's son had been my friend the year before, but he didn't want to meet Jesus or come to church. He even started making fun of me. I could handle him, as we were both just twelve years old. But this kid's dad was our football coach, and he started chiding me, cussing at me, and mocking me because of my faith in Jesus.

My dad was out of town when this all started. When he got home, I told him about it, and he said he'd take care of it. Keep in mind that this coach was big and my dad was pretty much medium-sized. Well, I'm not sure exactly what transpired, but suffice it to say, that guy never picked on me again. In fact, he never spoke to me again.

Wow, did my dad cause me to feel safe. He just took care of business when I let him know what was going on in my life. I could share many more stories like that—times he made sure I felt safe. I also saw him do the same for my sister and my mom. He took time to be with us, to listen to us, and then respond to what we needed.

In CaveTime, this is the type of prayer relationship you can have with your heavenly Father. A conversational one. Stone 3, prayer, is a powerful weapon to help you deal with the assaults and pressures coming your way.

Of course, I didn't even think about it when I was a boy. But now I know how much it would have hurt my dad if I waited at the door on Fridays, asked for the present he almost always got me, said thanks, and then took off without saying another word until I asked him for a present the next time he came home. Yet that's how many men pray— they look to the Father as someone who just takes care of their needs, so they bring lists of needs to Him.

"Hey God, could You take care of giving me enough money to pay the bills?"

"God, my kid has a cold. Could You heal him for me?"

"God, my wife is nagging me about cleaning the garage. Could You get her off of my back?"

"God, would You please move me up on the season ticket list? If You do, I'll drop an extra fifty bucks in the plate on Sunday."

"Hey God, one last thing. Would You please pay attention to the stock market a little better and have my mutual fund get a better rate next quarter? Thanks."

Of course, these kinds of prayers don't make us a wall for our people. Even more basic, this certainly would not be pursuing a relationship with Jesus. These kinds of requests make God out to be some type of heavenly Walmart, Costco, or Sam's Club.

Instead, let's show up, worship, and then have some powerful conversations with Him.

David's Model

Let's look at how David used the stone of prayer. As you begin to use this tool, I have no doubt that you will become very effective at slinging the stone of prayer at the giants assaulting your life.

God was a Dad with whom David could be very real.

David had to be real. He and God spoke often. He would know if David lied. David and his Father knew each other's names. He practiced being completely transparent with God, without the risk of rejection. Of course, David couldn't be rejected because he was chosen. God had called him by the word of a prophet—a word that reached David in a field.

God wanted to speak with this young red-haired man. Maybe God had made his hair red so he'd stand out. They might have talked about it in one of their conversations. Red stood for fire. They would speak often about fire. They had a fiery faith in each other—David in God and God in David. The fire of their faith was sparked by a call, and fanned by the purposeful wind of the Spirit.

Here's the thing. God has called you, too. You have a purpose. And he calls you to learn and understand and carry out that purpose by having conversations with Him—with your Dad. He calls you to find your stones in the cave.

I'm not saying that David never asked God for anything. Of course he did. But his requests were usually part of a broader, deep, and continuing discussion with a God whom David knew deeply and wanted to know better. David brought a passion and intimacy to the worship of Yahweh that had not been seen in quite some time, if ever. He was real with God. They were close.[27]

Sometimes David was afraid and needed a Strong Tower. Sometimes he was angry and asked God to beat up some enemies (or maybe take care of an obnoxious coach). David expressed all of these issues and emotions to his Dad and asked Him to help him deal with them. Bottom line: David's relationship with God was much deeper than just wanting stuff from Him.

David wanted to *be with* God. He loved God passionately and wasn't afraid to say it. In fact, David often heaped praise and love and compliments upon his Dad. Here are just a few instances:

"I love you, LORD, my strength" (Psalm 18:1).

"The LORD is my Shepherd" (Psalm 23:1).

"The LORD is my light...my stronghold" (Psalm 27:1).

"I will extol the LORD at all times" (Psalm 34:1).

"O my Strength...O my Strength" (Psalm 59:9).

"I will praise your name forever and ever. Every day I will praise you" (Psalm 145:1-2).

I especially like that last one. It reminds me of grabbing my dad's leg as he came in the door from a trip and saying, "I missed you Dad, and I am never, ever, ever going to let you go."

As I waited by the door of our house for my dad, one of the first things I would do was tell him that I loved him. I wanted him to know it! And maybe my actions spoke louder than my words—waiting at the window and tackling him as he came in the door.

There was no doubt in God's mind that David loved Him deeply.

The Conversation

David is credited with writing at least half of the 150 Psalms in Scripture. His Psalms cover a myriad of topics. The Psalms are songs, poems, and prayers—and some are all three. In his words, David expressed praise, sadness, anger, fear, doubt, shame, jubilation, ecstasy, and the list goes on and on. My point is that no subject seemed to be off limits in David's conversations with God. And no emotion was deemed inappropriate. Dad wanted to hear it all.

Check out this list of just a few of the feelings that David expressed to his Dad, most of them taken from Psalms that are thought to have been written in the cave or about his experiences there:

"In my distress I called to the LORD" (18:6).

"I pursued my enemies and overtook them" (18:37).

"The LORD lives! Praise be to my Rock! Exalted be God my Savior!" (18:46).

"I will sing and make music to the LORD" (27:6).

"This poor man called and the LORD heard him" (34:6).

"Taste and see that the LORD is good" (34:8).

"My slanderers pursue me all day long" (56:2).

"When I am afraid, I will trust in you" (56:3).

"Have mercy on me, O God, have mercy on me" (57:1).

"O Lord God Almighty, the God of Israel, rouse yourself to punish all the nations; show no mercy to wicked traitors" (59:5).

"But do not kill them, O Lord our shield, or my people will forget. In your might, make them wander about and bring them down" (59:11).

"Look to my right and see, no one is concerned for me. I have no refuge; no one cares for my life" (142:4).

"I will exalt you, my God the King; I will praise your name for ever and ever" (145:1).

"The Lord is gracious and compassionate, slow to anger and rich in love. The Lord is good to all; He has compassion on all He has made" (145:8-9).

What a broad range of feelings David expressed openly and boldly in his prayers. He got angry. He got bitter. He was despondent and distressed. I think I even detect some hatred when he asked God not to kill his enemies—so that they might suffer more.

Have you ever had any of these feelings reverberate through you? I have. David was passionate about the power of God. In calmer moments he spoke of God's compassion, His grace, His love. The point is that David had real-life conversations with a real-life God.

A Three-Way Conversation

Prayer is also the stone where David and his men together entered into a conversation with the all-powerful God of the universe. I will delve into Stone 5, community, and the group element of CaveTime in Chapter 10. But it's important to realize that David prayed and had conversation with his men as well.

The times of prayer David had with his men might be the ultimate strategic move when it came to this army of Mighty-Men-in-the-making and their leader. As they hid in the cave, I'm sure they had conversations with each other. They got to know each other well as they talked about what they'd do after they came out of hiding. They would talk about their wives and their kids, their hopes and their dreams. Certainly, they reminisced about the good old days, and there were times of lament to each other and to God. And they had times of strategic planning as they set their minds upon what they were going to do to sustain themselves.

Sometimes when a new guy comes to a CaveTime for the first time, he might be taken aback by the fact that I don't usually open with a word of prayer and start an official Bible study. We almost always begin with worship music playing in the background while we have conversations about our week. Each guy eventually shares, and then at some point we enter into more formal prayer. I do feel, however, that there is a prayerful element to men sharing their hearts in transparent conversation before their God, in the cave. They are there. He is there. Prayer begins. Stone 3 is being used.

I am also certain that David and his men asked each other questions. They asked God questions. Sometimes they would respond to each other's questions, but other times they would just wait and let God do what only He could do through the power of prayerful silence.

Some mornings, I just sit in God's presence—in prayerful silence. Even when I gather with a group of men in the cave, there are times when we will get quiet and just let God have a quiet conversation with our souls, allowing Him to speak in ways too deep for words.

Have you ever heard the saying "The silence was almost deafening"? I believe this speaks of God shouting at us through times of prayerful silence. It is where and when your spirit hears things that your ears cannot. God speaks to your inner man and strategizes and prepares you for the relationships, interactions, actions, and battles that He sees on the horizon. There are things that only He can see from His eternal and time-unimpaired perspective, and sometimes He whispers them to you when you are quiet.

Conversations with each other and with God became the primary way the men in the cave communicated. As these men talked with each other and God, they got to know each other. They learned to trust each other. They came to love each other and were even willing to die for each other. Certainly, they got so close through these deep conversations that at times they just had to look at one another to get a point across.

I am guessing that sometimes these men used hand signals or made an unintelligible sound to convey a thought or direction. Their relationships went deeper than words because they had grown so close through their CaveTime conversations. Perhaps there were times when it was so dark that all they could do was make a sound like an animal for fear that they might be found out. But communication still took place.

A leader and his men, hiding, strategizing, gaining confidence, making sounds, making signals, conversing with each other and with God, often at the deepest levels. They entered into these closest of relationships. In the process, they were equipped and transformed to take on life.

That's how the stone of prayer is intended to work in our lives as well. Through prayerful conversations, God will help you and your brothers know where to be a wall for your people—how to stand for them and how to make them feel safe.

God is calling you to show up and have a conversation with Him. He wants to hear about your fears and your shame. He wants you to share your innermost feelings. He wants to hear what makes you happy and what makes you sad. He wants you to laugh and have a good laugh with you. He wants men to express their frustrations toward Him. Many guys don't allow themselves to do this because they think God is mad. God is not mad at you, and He is mature enough to handle your anger and anything that you want to say to Him. He wants to have a conversation.

God desires real, raw, and transparent relationships—ones that are forged in vibrant, truthful, prayer-filled conversations. Even if you are completely beaten up and so intimidated that all you can do is make a noise to God, make that noise! God wants to hear from you. He wants you to show up and try and speak with Him.

This is how giants are killed. Just start making noises to God. He interprets the noises you make. And then you can start to speak to God. He wants to hear about the details of your life. He wants to be told about your passions. He wants to hear specifics. He cares.

Three Stones, Two Roles

You've made some great progress in the cave. By this point, you are using Stone 1 (showing up), and you're beginning to function in Role 1 (having an individual relationship with God first). What's more, you are learning and understanding the value of just being with God. To be with God is life. It's a place where you can experience freedom from assaults, freedom from pressure, and freedom from performing.

You are also learning that you can look at God and have Him remove your shame simply by turning your face toward Him. He sets you free from condemnation and guilt. Stone 2, the stone of worship, helps you make that discovery. You realize that face-to-face interaction between an assaulted man and his God in worship restores and empowers you to shamelessly and boldly walk in your masculinity.

As you sense the restorative power that comes from being with God and looking at Him in worship, you more keenly sense the desire to speak with Him. You see this desire powerfully expressed by learning to use Stone 3, the stone of prayer. Having a transparent and authentic conversation with God gives you the opportunity to express Role 2, your masculine presence.

You understand the fact that you have X and Y chromosomes and are called to be—in fact, made to be—*the man* for the people in your world. Prayer affirms this. God created you to be a masculine presence on His behalf for the people in your world. And you now have the stones to do it.

Using Stone 3 means you understand the importance of having prayerful conversations with your heavenly Father. These conversations focus on the people in every aspect of your world. Hearing from God on their behalf and then putting into action what you've heard is actually living out Jesus' Great Proclamation that we would "be (His) witnesses in Jerusalem, and in all Judea and Samaria, and to the ends of the earth" (Acts 1:8). By engaging in prayer with God, you are walking in your masculine presence, *spiritually*, in the cave. As you do this, you'll find that God brings opportunities for you to walk *physically* in your masculine presence as well.

Escape the assaults. Hear from heaven. Go out and walk in your presence.

Long-Lasting Effects

I personally began to see the results of this type of prayer when I was just eighteen. I attended Arvada High School in Colorado. I graduated in 1980 and as a senior, I wanted to leave a lasting impression on my school.

I've always had a vision for souls. I remember praying by the flag-pole, way before it became a national movement. I also remember sharing my faith in the lunch room. But there was another event that I think probably had a more long-lasting effect. This event was kind of weird, but I am convinced that it made an impression, one that lasted thirty years.

The event was actually not unique to our youth group. In fact, it had been done before—several thousand years before. In Joshua 5-6, the Lord instructed the patriarch Joshua to lead his army on a march around the city of Jericho numerous times a day and for a certain number of days. This set off a movement of God that caused the walls of the city to fall and the army of God to win a great victory. While tumbling down the walls of Arvada High School wasn't our desired result, we assembled a group of about ten teenagers and our youth pastor to do a Jericho Walk around our school in 1980.

Of course, some scoffers watched. But I thought it was kind of cool. We even had to climb some locked fences and scale some small walls. I'm not sure what result we expected, but we did believe in faith that God would do something at our school. I know for certain that some of my friends accepted Jesus as Savior soon after our walk. Some of them went on to do great things for the Kingdom. I'm also sure that other believers in our school prayed for God to do things there as well. But I'm convinced that I was personally walking as a high school senior for something that occurred thirty years later.

After graduation in 1980, I went to college, Lori and I got married, and we moved back to Arvada. Over the next seven years, we lived in or around the Denver area with some ministry opportunities at my old school, but nothing of any great consequence (that I know of). In 1991, Lori and I moved our little family to Tulsa where we lived for the next seventeen years. Then, in 2008, we moved back to serve at a church in Arvada and finish up my doctoral work at Denver Seminary. For all we knew, we thought we might be living in that community for a long time.

Upon arriving in Arvada, I immediately went to my old school and began to meet the administrators, teachers, and students. I found that what was once an idyllic suburb in the western part of the metro Denver area had become a transitional area, with many of the problems faced by other cities in our nation. Crime was up. Drug usage, vandalism, and gang activity were also on the rise. I also learned that Arvada High School had the largest homeless teen population in the county.

Another major problem was that academically, the school had slipped to being one of the lowest and most underachieving schools in the county. After meeting the amazing teachers, administrators, and students, I knew that these issues didn't reflect what they were actually capable of.

Homeless teen population? One of the lowest academically in the county? In my hometown? No way! Gang violence in Arvada? I was shocked. This was my hometown, and I couldn't just sit there and watch. These people needed a wall.

I must admit that I was angry. I was mad at the enemy for assaulting this great place and its great people. I felt that I needed to exercise my masculine presence. I also felt a pull or leading that was "other than me"—as if a strategy had been predetermined and all I had to do was show up and be a man. I sensed God asking me to be His man at this particular time and place.

I set a meeting with the principal of Arvada High School at that time, Kathy Norton. Kathy is tied with my friend Tom O'Malley for the title of "Best High School Principal Ever," because the two of them have helped me develop a strategy for linking arms with local schools that has mobilized local communities of faith in powerful and miraculous fashion.

As I met with Kathy, I asked her what we might do as a local church to help her, the staff, and students. Without hesitation, she let us know that she had a large segment of students who couldn't afford the supplies to even start school; if we could provide those, it would be a huge help. As those who know me will confirm, I have a real gift of volunteering people to take action, especially the people who sit in the congregations at the churches where I serve.

Without flinching, I said we would take care of that for them, before even asking how many students might need supplies and how much it might cost. Suffice it to say, many students needed supplies and it was going to cost thousands of dollars to take care of them. Once again though, I must tell you that I felt as if this had already been handled— that the funds, the plan, and the results had been predetermined.

We just needed to show up.

The following Sunday, I stood in front of our church of several thousand people and mapped out the vision before them. We'd been asked to meet a real and very imminent need at a local school. I then said that I had already volunteered our church to meet the need. While minor snickering and uneasy shifting took place, they knew I was serious. They also knew they were going to be asked to give more of their time, treasure, and talent (in the middle of a bad recession in the U.S.).

I haven't read anywhere in Scripture that we can stop giving and doing when the economy is bad. So that didn't deter me. It didn't faze the great people in our church either, and they gave generously that day. They gave a lot of money and volunteered to bring school supplies to the church throughout the week as well. We showed up at Arvada High School with supplies to take care of every student who had a need, and we were also able to leave their staff with enough extra as students in need came to them.

This effort went so smoothly that Kathy was ready with her next request. This one had to do with our church supporting the school's football team. When I was in school, our football team was so good that hundreds of students regularly attended games, and we had even taken a state title. When Kathy came to us, the team had only won a couple of games over several years, and almost no one came to watch. This created a depressing situation for the athletes, their families, and for the overall school population.

What could we do?

Once again, I sensed that the solution had been preplanned and set in place. We simply started attending AHS football games as a church. We also bought their concessions and cheered, regardless of wins or losses. We sat in the stands and met the parents of the athletes and established relationships.

We also started a tradition for them. We started a group called the "Bulldog Backers" (as you can guess, the AHS mascot is a bulldog). The Backers wore special "Bulldog Backers" T-shirts. The group also provided a weekly restaurant-quality pregame meal at no charge to the school. Each of these actions was set in place in the context of a few weeks before and during the season. It was miraculous.

I wish I could say that it resulted in an undefeated season, but it didn't. However, it did result in bringing hope and light and life to a school and community. Our church became a wall for that school.

However, the crowning glory came for me personally when two things happened. First, after the last game of the season, the coach asked if we could host a banquet for the team at our church, as we had a sanctuary that was conducive to hosting big events. You know what I said, don't you? "Of course, my people would love to host it." I knew that we had an events coordinator, Leslie Reynolds, who was one of the most committed Bulldog Backers. In fact, she had been the point person for the weekly team dinners and often called the team "her boys."

Leslie became like the team mom. Of course she said yes, and the event was a production to honor "her boys" like you have never seen, paid for and staffed by the Bulldog Backers. It was a magical night, and those athletes, coaches, and families who came to our church will forever remember that some of God's people stood for them as a wall, regardless of wins and losses.

Lori and I no longer serve at the church where this all began, but the Bulldog Backers live on. The leadership of the church where I served lost the vision for that school, the students who attend there, and the staff and administrators. But that didn't matter. Under the direction of one of the original Backers, Brandon Walker, the group incorporated and continues to serve the AHS population and stand as a wall for them.

God's plans supersede the decisions or indecisions of men every time. But this was all set in motion years before—I am convinced of it.

As I've said, I believe this effort at AHS was predetermined and set in motion years earlier. I have no doubt it was. Remember the Jericho Walk I was a part of in 1980? I am convinced that it was one of the major catalysts that set these successes in motion.

Of course, I don't mean to imply that I was the only one involved in those prayer events as a high school senior. But I do know that as I spent time in my cave, thirty years after standing by that flagpole and after walking around that school and actively sharing my faith, God let me know that He had credited and focused those prayers beyond what we saw in 1980. He had been planning for this time in history. As I stood as a wall then, He would orchestrate, move, and synthesize prayers to prompt the events of people's lives and the battle between darkness and light. He did all this to see His Kingdom come and His will be done at AHS.

Using the stone of prayer and walking in my masculine presence as a young man, I was involved in an event that prepared the way for me to stand as a wall and see mighty things happen in that same place as a forty-nine-year-old.

The power of the stone of prayer: an eternal conversation, responding to today's assaults, and becoming a wall for those around you and generations to come.

Note: Just as I did with the two previous stones, I have provided some additional ideas on making the most of your times in prayer. If you need help getting started in a time of wonderful conversation with your heavenly Dad, I urge you to go to "Strap on the Toolbelt: Tools for Practicing the Stones," at the end of this book and make use of the additional tools provided there.

*In God, whose word I praise,
in the LORD, whose word I praise—
in God I trust and am not afraid.
What can man do to me?
I am under vows to you, my God;
I will present my thank offerings to you.
For you have delivered me from death
and my feet from stumbling,
that I may walk before God
in the light of life.*

—Psalm 56:10-13

*The Word of God goes to the very center of who
we are. It cuts through to that which bonds us
together as a being; it touches upon that which
forms the essence of who we are.*

—Robert Mulholland

Chapter 9

STONE 4: *WORD*

A s I sit here right now, I'm holding the Bible that started the process of me becoming a man of the Word. It's a little brown Gideon Bible that my dad gave me on January 31, 1974. My name and the date are written on the inside. I was eleven-and-a-half years old. In June of that same year, I went on a backpacking trip that forever changed my life. And that Bible went with me.

This was my first real backpacking trip. I was in Colorado's Gore Wilderness Area with a group of about ten other packers and our leaders, who were amazing outdoorsmen. On the first day, they told us that we should never go off by ourselves—not even to go to the bathroom. I'm sure they went over other rules, such as always carrying a whistle to use in the unlikely event we ever got lost. With a whistle, if you got lost, you stayed in one spot and blew your whistle and yelled.

I quickly filed that information somewhere in the recesses of my competitive mind. I figured I'd remember rules like that after I beat everyone else up the mountain.

The first two days were awesome, but by day three I was tired of the slow pace. I had also convinced a couple of other packers that we should start out early and be the first to the next camp site. Against his better judgment, our leader eventually relented to my pleas and let us go ahead of the group, instructing us that whenever we got to a fork in the trail, we should turn right. Yes! We were going to be the first up the mountain. We would win.

There we were: three twelve-year-olds, in the rugged Colorado Rockies, trying to be the first ones up the mountain, following a trail we didn't know. About an hour in, we realized that we'd actually run out of trail and were on a game trail. Game trails aren't actual National Forest Service trails, but trails used by various animals to feed and travel to sources of water.

In about another thirty minutes, we realized that we were lost. I might have been the first of the three to start yelling for my mom, but the other two eventually joined in.

In our panic, we were about to break all of the rules that raise the chances of being found alive. We didn't sit and wait for our leaders. We walked in circles and then backtracked.

Through a series of several more mistakes, our group of three got separated. In the rugged wilderness of Colorado were three individual, scared twelve-year-olds, very lost.

Death was on my mind. Would I be killed by a bear, a mountain lion, or just freeze to death?

God's Word Made Real

I decided that I wasn't going to just wait and die sitting down, so I began to walk toward a high mountain ridge that looked familiar. It was Eliot's Ridge. As I ascended out of the little bowl where Mirror Lake sits below Eagles' Nest, I began to recognize a trail on the side of the mountain. We had been down that trail two days earlier, and it was a long way back to where we started. But I knew there would be people at the trailhead—people with food and people who could take me to my parents.

As I began to walk, I felt something in my shirt pocket. I patted my chest and realized it was the little brown Gideon New Testament. Our family had only recently become followers of Jesus, so we hadn't been Christians long enough to know many verses. But my parents had become radical disciples, and we'd been having family devotions and going to church together. I'd learned from my parents and my youth group leaders that God still spoke to people through His Word.

What the heck? I thought to myself. It was worth a try. So I opened the Bible, and in the back of it my dad had highlighted some verses.

Two of those verses had saved my eternal soul just months earlier, but they took on a new significance at nearly 12,000 feet. The first verse was John 3:16. I read it, and as a physically lost twelve-year-old, it came alive! The verse was written right there on the last page of the Gideon Bible, in KJV English, and I am reading out of it right now:

> For God so loved the world, that He gave His only begotten Son, that whosoever believeth in Him should not perish, but have everlasting life (KJV).

I then scanned down to the last verse my dad had written on that page; it was from Paul's epistle to the Romans:

> For whosoever shall call on the name of the Lord, shall be saved (Romans 10:13, KJV).

As I said, I had been saved spiritually only months earlier. Now those words jumped off of the page at me: "Whosoever believeth in Him should not perish" and "Whosoever shall call on the name of the Lord shall be saved." Those words from God's Word were mine, right then and there.

At that moment, I let God know that I wanted those words to be true for me right then, not just eternally. In faith, on Eliot's Ridge, I stood on those verses. Suddenly, they weren't just ancient words for ancient people. I would not perish and I knew it. God spoke to me and I knew it. I know it now! I would be saved, and God would guide me. His Word guaranteed it!

You can tell me how my reasoning was bad theology, and that John 3:16 and Romans 10:13 apply to our spiritual condition. But God spoke to me through them that day as a full-of-faith twelve-year-old. My respect for the Word of God came alive. And almost thirty-eight years later, it's more alive now than ever.

Almost immediately I felt a peace—a calm that wasn't there earlier. I walked out of a very perilous situation there in the Gore. But I wasn't alone. I had the living Word of God guiding me.

God also called me into the ministry on that day. As we traveled together, we had a lengthy conversation about life, ministry, fear, family, wilderness, mountains, and my future. When we were done talking, I knew that God wanted me to become a pastor. He called me to serve Him by taking care of His people. I felt humbled and weird and secure and guided by God.

Walking with Sheep

An interesting aspect to this story that I didn't know at the time screams at me now as a profound confirmation of my time with God.

Back in the 1970s, shepherds used some of the high mountain meadows as open range for grazing their sheep. We had discovered this on the first day of our trip when we crested a hill that led into an alpine meadow. As we came to the top of that hill, we found ourselves among a huge flock of sheep. I was there, standing among sheep, shepherds, sheep dogs, and tents. It was an awesome sight.

I am still blown away by the connection I see now. Here it is: God refers to His people as sheep. He is their Great Shepherd. Jesus refers to Himself in John 10 as the Good Shepherd who lays down His life for His sheep. I know without a doubt that our Great Shepherd was giving me a picture of what He had in store for my life. There I was walking among sheep at age twelve—the very thing that I would eventually spend the rest of my life doing.

Walking with sheep. Tending sheep. Being a pastor.

God's Word lit my path, led me out of a perilous time, inspired faith in me on a rocky trail there in the Rockies, and called me into my destiny. Over the years, when the road hasn't been easy—and as the assaults have come with their accompanying thunder and lightning—I have held tightly to that experience with His Word.

A conversation with God on Eliot's Ridge, walking with Him, and walking with sheep.

Just as God spoke to me in the mountains all of those years ago, I believe He wants to speak to all of us. David knew to go to the cave and hear from his Lord. In my head, I know where to go too. That's why after my ER experience, I knew that God would speak. I didn't know exactly how, or what the word would be, but I knew He would give me direction. God is a good shepherd and He shepherds me the same way He had shepherded David and his men.

Would you like God to shepherd you? Would you like to have a plan to deal with issues that plague you—the assaults and attacks waged against you? Good.

The plan might be right in front of you, just like the little Gideon Bible I am still holding now. The plan is God's Word. Yes, God provided this Word thousands of years ago, but it's also provided for your life today.

You can use God's Word like a sling, and giants will die.

David and Sheep

David was a shepherd. One of the most famous chapters in all of Scripture is his Psalm 23. In this Psalm, David describes the relationship a shepherd has with his sheep. Each sheep relies on knowing the voice of the shepherd, listening for it, and then responding accordingly. If the sheep doesn't respond, it could mean death or serious injury.

I have a good friend named Steve Roper. Steve has done many things, including being a shepherd. He told me about a time when he was showing his sheep at the Oklahoma State Fair and his lamb was in a pen with a flock of sheep. The flock was comprised of many sheep from many different flocks. Many unique people around, many noises, many sheep, and many shepherds made the situation potentially very confusing to all parties involved.

Steve said he had spent much time with this lamb. He talked with it, stroked its wool, cleaned it, fed it, and medicated it. He really loved that lamb. But how would his lamb respond in all of this confusion? It was their first show.

So Steve walked up to the fence, called his lamb's name in the midst of all the clamor, and immediately the sheep's head popped up out of the flock and looked to find where Steve's voice had come from. It then began to bleat, making its way to Steve as quickly as possible. It instinctively wanted to be touched and spoken to by him.

That conversation with Steve helped me to see Psalm 23 in a new light. The words are familiar to many people, but here it is to remind you:

> The LORD is my shepherd, I lack nothing. He makes me lie down in green pastures, he leads me beside quiet waters, he refreshes my soul. He guides me along the right paths for his name's sake. Even though I walk through the darkest valley, I will fear no evil, for you are with me; your rod and your staff, they comfort me. You prepare a table before me in the presence of my enemies. You anoint my head with oil; my cup overflows. Surely your goodness and love will follow me all the days of my life, and I will dwell in the house of the LORD forever (Psalm 23:1-6).

David uses the metaphor of God being his shepherd in these verses. But we often forget that David's experience with shepherding was first-hand, with his own animals. So David is describing what he had done for his sheep.

Steve shared that he was the sole caregiver for his lamb. He fed it, protected it, and medicated it. In Psalm 23:1, David speaks of this type of shepherd-sheep relationship by saying, "I lack nothing." Just like David's own sheep lacked nothing, God took total care of David.

Steve gave me new perspective with his experience at the fair. He helped me see that the animal knew and trusted his voice. His voice had called the sheep to rest and to be fed and watered. David speaks of this in verse 3: "He makes me to lie down in green pastures, He leads me beside still waters." The shepherd's voice meant food, water, safety, and all good things. His voice also called the sheep to be medicated. This is the concept presented in verse 5: "He anoints my head with oil." In David's day, this would have been medicinal oil that had a cooling effect on skin irritations and kept away pests like flies and ticks.

The voice of the shepherd calling the sheep to come and be healed.

Finally, the shepherd's voice called the sheep to come into the safety of the fold and sleep without fear of predators. In verse 6, David speaks of the power of this type of peace and security: "I will dwell in the house of the Lord forever." No fear. As a good shepherd takes care of his sheep, God will take care of us.

What an awesome picture. God is our shepherd. He speaks to us. He spoke to David in the cave. He spoke to me in the mountains. And He will speak to you too.

A Light in the Dark

When David escaped to the cave, he obviously didn't have electricity. So there were no bright lights. I imagine that David and the 400 had lanterns and candles. But they very likely knew what total darkness looked and felt like.

In Psalm 18, David gives another description about what happens when you allow the Word of God to direct you. Not only is it like a shepherd's voice, guiding you into safety, provision, and a life of fearlessness. God's Word is also a light in darkness, illumination from another world. This Psalm was likely written after the assaults from Saul and other enemies had ceased. David describes the power of God's Word to sustain in darkness and provide a way out of it:

> You, LORD, keep my lamp burning; my God turns my darkness into light. With your help I can advance against a troop; with my God I can scale a wall. As for God, his way is perfect: The LORD's word is flawless; he shields all who take refuge in him. For who is God besides the LORD? And who is the

Rock except our God? It is God who arms me with strength and keeps my way secure. He makes my feet like the feet of a deer; he causes me to stand on the heights. ...You provide a broad path for my feet, so that my ankles do not give way (Psalm 18:28-33; 36).

My hope is that you and I arrive at the place David did. In this place, we realize that God does speak. His words can help turn your darkness and confusion about the situations that you face into light. His Word can illumine you as you seek truth from it in the cave.

His Word can help you deal with relational problems and financial barriers that seem insurmountable, and you can "scale a wall" (Psalm 18:29). And His Word will give you direction to walk out of the wilderness where you find yourself: "a broad path for my feet, so that my ankles do not give way" (Psalm 18:36). Not only can you walk out of your wilderness, but you don't have to sprain an ankle.

Even though I was just twelve years old, I still vividly remember how it felt physically to walk out of my wilderness experience. I had faith in God's Word. I didn't just stand on it, I walked on it. Although I felt a bit tired when I was eventually found, I didn't even come close to spraining my ankle. God's Word is His confirming and directing voice to you and me each day.

The Harvard School of Communications conducted a study, trying to identify as many ways to communicate as possible. They found more than 700,000![28] Amazing isn't it? This means many, many ways exist for someone to communicate with you. That includes God. However, we always need to remember that God will never contradict His Word contained in the Bible. Anything He communicates to us will always confirm Scripture. That's why we must regularly interact with God's Word—to hear His voice, to learn how to recognize it, and to understand how to best use this stone.

The Word in the Cave

David and his men didn't bring their Bibles with them as they fled for their lives to the cave. Yet David wrote in Psalm 18:30 that "the word of the Lord" is "flawless." The Word was with them in the cave. I'm sure David had portions of the Pentateuch memorized, hidden, and inscribed upon his heart. So the Word was present in his life, and I'm sure he spoke it to himself and to his men. As a result, he was built up in faith for the mission God had for him—whatever that was.

David was also waiting for a fresh word from heaven—a word of deliverance and direction. Whenever he received that word, he downloaded it to his men, and then they would implement it.

David showed up to the cave knowing he would receive a word from the Lord. He was committed to staying there until "I learn what God will do for me" (1 Samuel 22:3). While he didn't know when a word would come or what it would be, he knew that it *would* come. And when this information from his faithful God came, David would act. He would form, conform, and transform himself and his troops to what that word for "right now" said.

The comparisons to our lives as men today are screaming out, aren't they? In order to know how and where to stand as a wall, a man needs to have marching orders. The living Word of God for men, right now, contains those marching orders. God still speaks, and He still visits men under assault as they hide in their caves. This direction from God instructs us on when to fight and when to hide.

The lives of David and his men were a series of times of hiding and fighting, hiding and fighting. A rhythm of life and time.

The rhythm of CaveTime.

Note: As with the previous stones, look for ideas on making the most of your time interacting with God's Word in "Strap on the Toolbelt: Tools for Practicing the Stones," at the end of this book. I encourage you to make use of the tools provided there.

I will extol the Lord at all times;
his praise will always be on my lips.
I will glory in the Lord;
let the afflicted hear and rejoice.
Glorify the Lord with me;
let us exalt his name together.

—Psalm 34:1-3

A man of a right spirit is not a man of narrow
and private views, but is greatly interested and
concerned for the good of the community to which
he belongs, and particularly of the city or village
in which he resides, and for the true welfare of
the society of which he is a member.

—Jonathan Edwards

Chapter 10

STONE 5: *COMMUNITY*

Just yesterday, I caught myself saying to my wife, Lori: "It's a man thing, you just wouldn't understand."

She promptly responded: "I'm sure I wouldn't, and I'm thinking that I might not want to!"

I can also recall times when she said to me: "It's a woman thing," prompting the same response from me.

In the Introduction, we looked briefly at why differences exist between men and women. One isn't "better" than the other. Men aren't of greater value than women or vice versa. We simply have different roles.

Because God wired us to have different roles in life, there are just things that men and women will never be able to understand about each other. However, that is no excuse to write off the other gender. In fact, we should see these role differences as an invitation to pursue potentially very powerful relationships—to value the differences and pursue a relationship with one another.

The Power of Relationship

Consider the following three verses. In just these few words you can find a biblical foundation for understanding the power of relationships, "the man thing," and how it fits into the whole CaveTime process.

Then God said, "Let us make mankind in our image, in our likeness, so that they may rule over the fish in the sea and the birds in the sky, over the livestock and all the wild animals, and over all the creatures that move along the ground" (Genesis 1:26).

How the mighty have fallen in battle! Jonathan lies slain on your heights. I grieve for you, Jonathan my brother; you were very dear to me. Your love for me was wonderful, more wonderful than that of women (2 Samuel 1:25-26).

Though one may be overpowered, two can defend themselves. A cord of three strands is not quickly broken (Ecclesiastes 4:12).

In the first reference, although some translations use the word "man," we need to understand that God is talking about mankind or all of humanity. We need to remember that both sexes have God's imprint on them. They are valuable and important.

Notice that as God speaks in this verse, He does so in the plural: "Let *us* make mankind in *our* image, in *our* likeness." I believe that this is one of the earliest references to the Trinity. God shows us that He is a relationship within Himself. God the Father, God the Son, and God the Holy Spirit.

God values relationships. He is one! He also made men and women, individual human beings He could relate to. When God knows and relates with us, it gives Him pleasure and fulfills our purpose.

In a similar way, a power is present when we know each other as humans in healthy and appropriate ways, because these relationships reflect the nature of God in us. Because all of our relationships can be complicated and complex, I like to call the healthy ways we know and relate to each other by a simple term: living well.

When we act like God in our relationships, we can't go wrong. This is what Stone 5, community, is all about. This stone propels a man into operating in Role 3, the pursuit of relationships that help him to live well. These relationships will be pursued with both men and women, by men who are married, and by men who are single.

Living Well, with Women

How can a man operate in Role 3 with the women in his life? Another way to ask the question would be: "How can a man live well with the women in his life?"

First, let's think about this question for men who are married. If you're a married man, the best way for you to fully express the image of God in your world is to have a healthy relationship with your wife. Be a wall for her! Protect her, defend her, and be a place of comfort and grace for her.

How can you accomplish this? First, consider the advice offered by the apostle Paul as a foundation for your marriage:

> Husbands, love your wives, just as Christ also loved the church and gave Himself for her, that He might sanctify and cleanse her with the washing of water by the word (Ephesians 5:25-26).

This is pretty straightforward. You are to lay down your life for your wife.

Even as I write this, I feel convicted. Many times I don't do this well (of course, there are times when I do). I must admit though, as I get older, I am starting to get this one. Bottom line: If you're married and want to live well, pursue Stone 5 and get some healthy community going with your wife.

Love your wife like Jesus loved the church. He died for it. He gave His life for it. For men, it all starts here. If you want to love Jesus more, love your wife more! Die for her. Put your desires after hers. When you do this, you will be moving in the direction of living well in your marriage.

Living Well, with Men

What does it mean to live well with the men in our lives? What is healthy community for men—the kind that helps us to live well?

I think that David knew a thing or two about a band of brothers. He had 400 brothers in the cave. He also had experienced a close relationship with Jonathan, the son of King Saul. We spoke of this earlier, but let's take another look at how David described their friendship, in the lament he sang after hearing of Jonathan's death:

> I grieve for you, Jonathan my brother; you were very dear to me. Your love for me was wonderful, more wonderful than that of women (2 Samuel 1:26).

There is some powerful language in this one verse. David describes what I was trying to convey to Lori when I said, "It's a man thing."

A power and synergy exists between men that is indescribable unless you possess the X and Y and have experienced it. David used the term "wonderful" to speak of the fact that Jonathan loved him. This was an unconditional love that preferred David above Jonathan's own interests. This love superseded fraternal love. These guys were best friends, and they would give their lives for one another if necessary.

Powerful, isn't it? This is the type of healthy relationship that brings out honor, integrity, and the best in a man. Living well and being a wall for those in his care.

In this verse, David uses the term "wonderful" again. He says that the love he and Jonathan had was "more wonderful" than that of women. Some commentators, as well as the Targum (the Aramaic translations of the Old Testament), point toward a phrase that more correctly says, "more than the love of two women." So, the actual verse would sound something like this: "Your love for me was wonderful, more wonderful than the love of both of my wives combined."[29]

David had two wives at the time he wrote these lines. And although his wives loved him, the type of love he felt for Jonathan was more powerful. David is not referring to any kind of sexual or romantic love. He is talking about a relationship that was deep and helped the participants to live well. The healthy and masculine relationship between David and Jonathan was an example of a powerful community.

Stone 5 (community) being honed, as Role 3 (pursuing healthy relationships that allow each party to be built up and fully alive) was taking place.

Living Well with a Group of Men

I believe there is one other type of masculine relationship that men can experience. It's spoken of in the third Scripture we read above, Ecclesiastes 4:12:

> Though one may be overpowered, two can defend themselves.
> A cord of three strands is not quickly broken.

While this verse doesn't speak only of masculine relationships, it does speak of the relational synergy that can be experienced among a band of brothers. A man and his friend can stand back to back, defending each other from a rear assault. However, three men can see attacks coming from every direction. A synergy occurs when a third man of equal commitment is added to the mix. The resulting force is more powerful than the sum of the parts: 1 + 1 + 1 does not equal 3, but much more than 3. What an awesome power and force. When men of equal commitment enter into a relationship with one another, they can do powerful and amazing feats.

Fireteams. Beginning with the Trinity, the concept of a relational team is foundational in the Bible. I guess King Solomon knew a thing or two about them when he wrote about a cord with three strands not being quickly or easily broken. The context seems to speak of warfare—or at least some type of contest.

Solomon probably witnessed this relational cord among men as he watched his father, David. David had his most trusted friends, who were bound by a deep, powerful, and masculine love. Solomon had probably heard of David's deep love for his friend, Jonathan, or had seen or heard firsthand accounts of their miraculous exploits. Whatever the case, Solomon knew the power of men in focused relationships—bands of brothers creating a wall of men.

David even based the structure and spirit of his army on his understanding of brotherhood set into a context of warfare. His men shared a kindred spirit—a love and trust that would be honed in battle. They became legendary, transitioning from 400 nameless men escaping from their demons into David's Mighty Men.

Small units of men, together doing huge things.

The units were broken up into teams of three and thirty, and we even know some of their names:

> Abishai the brother of Joab son of Zeruiah was chief of the *Three*. He raised his spear against *three* hundred men, whom he killed, and so he became as famous as the *Three*. Was he not held in greater honor than the Three? He became their commander, even though he was not included among them. Benaiah son of Jehoiada was a valiant fighter from Kabzeel, who performed great exploits. He struck down two of Moab's best men. He also went down into a pit on a snowy day and killed a lion. And he struck down a huge Egyptian. Although the Egyptian had a spear in his hand, Benaiah went against him with a club. He snatched the spear from the Egyptian's hand and killed him with his own spear. Such were the exploits of Benaiah son of Jehoiada; he too was as famous as the *three* mighty men. He was held in greater honor than any of the *Thirty*, but he was not included among the *Three*. And David put him in charge of his bodyguard (1 Chronicles 11:18-23, emphasis added).

My son Jacob learned much about teams of three when he was in boot camp and then combat training. I was fascinated as he told me about how these units of three trained and fought together. He and I talked at length about David's structure and how he had employed the small-team method as he built Israel's army. We pondered how David might have used and trained his teams of three.

As Jacob and I had a long conversation about this, he made a very powerful statement that I will never forget: "I'm sure that the fireteams were very effective and efficient for David and his men. They are for us. And if they were like Marines, I'm sure they killed with great accuracy. Dad, this fires me up and makes me want to go back to boot camp."

This made him want to go back to boot camp? Many describe the experience of boot camp as being like hell. I watched some of the new recruits at Jacob's graduation being "encouraged" by the drill instructors. It was brutal. But this group of men was going through hell with their brothers in arms, to whom they would be *Semper Fidelis* or "always faithful." The men in the Marine Corps are trained to live for this motto. In fact, they are trained to die for it.

With all of my heart, I want for the band of brothers who follow Jesus to feel this for one another as they fight for the cause of Christ—to be *Semper Fi* for one another.

I realized that if I could get into Jacob's head—in relation to the inner workings of these units—then I could get a glimpse into David's mind as well. I could gain some insight about how we might achieve some depth in the relationships that we men have with our brothers.

Jacob told me that the small units of three to four men are called fireteams in the Marine Corps. The Marine Corps fireteams are considered the most finely trained and tuned fighting force in the world.

Jacob was trained in the four-man model, which is made up of two teams of two. This legendary strategic team uses three protocols that I believe have direct application to CaveTime and Stone 5. If you apply these concepts in the CaveTime context, you'll be able to be involved in a fraternity of men that will be always faithful for Christ as you are *Semper Fidelis* for each other.

Stone 5, a community of brothers—a group of men who push you to live well.

Fireteam Protocol 1. Members never move alone, always in pairs, about ten feet apart. Each member is always covered and always covering someone. The teams of two never advance unless both are covered by fire and have a sufficient amount of ammo to move ahead, toward the target.

The practical application of this Fireteam Protocol to a CaveTime group would be that members should always cover each other in prayer during the week. No movement into a day without prayer. Although you might not meet every day as a group, you will pray for each other every day. A band of brothers constantly praying for each other.

No man left un-prayed for.

A rule that I have instituted with all of my CaveTime groups is: "Unless I cancel CaveTime, we will always have it." I still communicate with my guys each week. But they know that CaveTime will be consistent and never cancelled unless I notify them. This keeps CaveTime as a constant in their lives—constantly there for security and accountability. Each man knows the other guys will be there waiting on him and thinking about him. And if for some reason he can't come, they will be praying for him.

I asked Tim, one of my theology students who started his own CaveTime group at school, to describe what CaveTime has brought to his life. He immediately fired back: "Brotherhood...the value of brotherhood."

He said. "We pray, we read the Bible. We are real about our own stuff...raw and authentic. Two other guys who are hungry for this are the ones who come every week." Tim is a great leader, pouring himself into the lives of the guys in his dorm at school.

What confidence would you have if you knew that your brother—or a group of brothers—was praying for you daily? Just like covering fire, prayers from a brother can help you stand as a wall for your family. These prayers can help you stand at your place of work and as you make major decisions. These prayers can empower you to move ahead with confidence at the right time, knowing you will reach your destination or hit the desired target of your prayers because you are covered.

Fireteam Protocol 2. Members of the fireteams trust implicitly that each soldier will do his job.

Each fireteam member has a specific job and his members trust him implicitly to get his job done. The practical application of this Fireteam Protocol to a CaveTime group is that each member of the group will be responsible for a particular element of the cave each week. Everyone will bring Stone 1 (showing up). One member might bring Stone 2 (leading and being responsible for worship). The number of members in your group dictates how many stones each member needs to bring.

The point is that when you have a group of brothers wholeheartedly committed to their CaveTime and bringing their stones each week, they will undoubtedly be changed. They will be held accountable to be *Semper Fi* to their brothers.

Fireteam Protocol 3. Team members communicate with each other often. In the Marines, this is done verbally as well as with code words, timing, and signals. The men practice communicating often and in different settings. This assures that during battle conditions, team members won't be surprised.

The practical application of this Fireteam Protocol to a CaveTime group is that each member will communicate with another member each week. This could be by text, email, phone call, or in person. Regular communication is vital to the success of the cave, providing encouragement and accountability. It also acts as an information-gathering mechanism so that prayer cover can be current and focused.

Jacob's insights were invaluable. I'm convinced that as you become involved in CaveTime with brothers who practice Stone 5 with the fervor of Marines in a fireteam, your lives will change. Men will become walls. Families will be safe and secure. Communities in turmoil will be filled with hope. Areas that were once crime-riddled will be put on notice by men of prayer and action.

Community and life—living in synergy with some other brothers—
a band of brothers living well together.

Addicted to the Rhythm of the Cave

I know that the word addicted can have bad connotations. But I
can't think of a better term to describe what has happened in my life
with the other men I have met with in the cave.

I have to hear God's voice. I need to have a conversation with Him.
I must have Him speak clearly to me. For me, I have had these things
happen in the cave—over and over and over again, for many years.
You might say they've become a rhythm of life for me.

I've realized that I need this rhythm because the attacks and lightning bolts come just as rhythmically.

The enemy is relentless, so we must be as well.

*Note: For some practical steps on living well—for pursuing, main-
taining, developing, and expanding healthy relationships for and with the
people in your life—I urge you to check out and make use of the tools
provided in "Strap on the Toolbelt: Tools for Practicing the Stones," at the
end of this book.*

Lord, my shepherd strong
You lead me on
A table's before me, among my enemies
Anoint my head
Surely Your love and goodness shall follow
All of my days, I will dwell here
All of my days

"Shepherd Strong" by David Gungor and John Arndt
From *CaveTime: The Escape, A Worship Experience*

They died hard, those savage men—like wounded
wolves at bay. They were filthy, and they were
lousy, and they stunk. And I loved them.

—Douglas MacArthur

Chapter 11

PICK A FIGHT: *BUT PICK* *THE RIGHT ONE*

I absolutely love the phrase, "Pick a fight."

I don't know whether he said it or not, but some believe Scotland's great emancipator, William Wallace, said, "I'm going to pick a fight!" to his ragged and painted up Scottish troops. These incensed men had questioned Wallace about his intentions pertaining to the army facing them on the other side of the battle-field at Stirling Bridge in 1297.

The army was that of King Edward I of England, who was also called Longshanks. After stating that he was going to pick that fight, Wallace commenced doing so by charging his horse across the field, demanding that the English—who occupied Scotland at that time—surrender, lay down their arms, and leave Scotland immediately. Initially, the English army was amused but then promptly insulted as the Scots followed Wallace's commands with foul language and obscene gestures pointed in their direction.

Offended, Longshanks' troops engaged the Scots and got their tails soundly kicked. I would say Mr. Wallace picked the right fight, even though it proved to be long and bloody and eventually cost him and many of his men their lives. However, because Wallace picked the right fight, Scotland eventually gained its freedom from England.

We men love a great storyline like this one that was portrayed in *Braveheart*. I saw the movie *Gladiator* five times when it came out. The first time, I jumped up in a packed theater and yelled in support of Maximus as he engaged in hand-to-hand combat with a series of gladiators while the evil little cheat Caesar—who had just stabbed him with a dagger he'd hidden in his cloak—looked on. My heart is starting to race a bit right now as I remember it.

I'm a total sucker for movies like these, where a hero stands up against the bad guy and takes a shot at him against all odds.

Whether it is Maximus in *Gladiator*, William Wallace on the fields of Scotland, John Wayne as Rooster Cogburn facing off against Lucky Ned Pepper and his gang, Davey Crockett and Colonel Travis at the Alamo, the Marines at Iwo Jima, or the men who hit the beaches at Normandy, these stories touch me at my core. Even the ones that aren't true touch me. I think that most guys want to be Wallace, Cogburn, Crockett, or Maximus.

I believe that we men are simply hardwired that way. What's more, because you are wired that way, you *can* be those guys! Right there at Stirling Bridge, in the Amphitheaters, and on the sands of Iwo Jima in your world!

Because we possess the X and Y chromosomes, we just can't help ourselves. We want to be *the man*. God created you to be *the man* in your world and in various spheres of influence.

You were created to pick the right fight in those places as well!

Picking the Right Fight

We'll look at Jesus more closely in Chapter 13. But the following verse tells of Jesus being led by the Spirit into battle.

> At once the Spirit sent him out into the wilderness, and he was in the wilderness forty days, being tempted by Satan. He was with the wild animals, and angels attended him (Mark 1:12-13).

Jesus knew that not every fight was His—just the ones given to Him. In John 17:4, He says:

> I have brought you glory on earth, by completing the work you gave me to do.

Jesus picked the right fights—the ones that God gave Him. These included fights with the Gadarene demoniac (Matthew 8:28); the Pharisees (too many to count); with the money changers in the Temple (Matthew 21:12); with the men who were about to stone an adulteress (John 8:1); and ultimately the one with the sons of the world on the cross. When He fought this last fight, in victory He proclaimed, "It is finished" (John 19:30).

David also knew what to do when it came to picking the right fights. First, he sought God's direction:

> The prophet Gad said to David, "Do not stay in the stronghold. Go into the land of Judah." So David left and went to the forest of Hereth...When David was told, "Look, the Philistines are fighting against Keilah and are looting the threshing floors," he inquired of the LORD, saying, "Shall I go and attack these Philistines?" The LORD answered him, "Go, attack the Philistines and save Keilah" (1 Samuel 22:5; 23:1-2).

In 1 Samuel 22:5, David had a prophetic word from the prophet Gad. And in 1 Samuel 23:2, he received a direct word from God. In both of these instances, God had a clear-cut direction for David to head.

We also have specific fights that belong only to us. These fights will come onto our radar, and making sure we've had our CaveTime allows us to identify the right fights. And when it's time to fight, we can say with William Wallace, "I'm going to pick a fight!"

Using the Right Weapons

Not every man will fight like William Wallace did. And I'm not saying that you will need to be physically violent. I am trying to convey that because you are a man, God has equipped you to stand in some manner. I believe this is inevitable, and if you have been in the cave, you will be up to the task. Through CaveTime, you will know when and how to be ready.

As a possessor of the X and Y, God equips you to fight for the people He has given you to stand for. Husbands for wives. Fathers for sons and daughters. All men to stand for those who look to you for physical and spiritual protection.

You will even be called to stand for those who have no one else to stand for them. This is just what men do—it's what we were designed for. You'll find these people at your workplace, in local schools, in nursing homes, on the streets, and in the halls of government.

Like the following examples, you are called to stand in unique and powerful ways.

Fighting for Forty-Four Years

For every William Wallace, there is a William Wilberforce. The son of a wealthy merchant, he became a member of British Parliament in 1780 at the young age of twenty-one.

In his early years, Wilberforce was a "player," as we would say in American culture. He was a womanizer, hard drinker, and totally self-indulgent. However, he met Jesus in 1790 and became profoundly changed. As a result of his radical conversion, he knew that he was called to stand as a wall and fight for social reform, with his initial stand on the behalf of British factory workers.

His most famous and memorable stand, which has been commemorated in the powerful movie *Amazing Grace*, was against slavery in Britain. Wilberforce didn't attack militarily. Instead, he relentlessly introduced antislavery legislation in Parliament—for eighteen years in a row—and finally saw the institution abolished in 1807. However, this didn't free people who were already slaves. So Wilberforce continued to stand as a wall and fight for all of them. He didn't see ultimate victory until just before his death in 1833.

Led of God, Wilberforce picked the right fight. Although it took forty-four years, he was victorious. Wilberforce was a long-standing wall.

The Fight for Masculine Presence

Another man led of God to pick the right fight is Tom O'Malley. I referred to him earlier, but I want to fill in some more details. Tom is a longtime friend of mine who was a teacher, coach, and school administrator for more than thirty years.

When Tom told me he planned to retire, I knew it wouldn't last long because Tom loves kids. He is perhaps the most knowledgeable and effective public educator I've ever met.

Right after his "retirement," I asked Tom if he would go to the local school closest to our church and ask the principal, Tamara Bird, if our church could do anything to help her, her students, and her staff. Without telling me specifically what she answered, Tom set up a meeting with Tamara so she could tell me herself. I referred to this meeting a few chapters ago; Tamara said that her students and staff needed a healthy masculine presence on their campus. They needed men to stand in the cafeteria and just be there during the day.

Tom said he would coordinate this effort. And he did. We recruited several other men, but Tom was in that cafeteria nearly every day. He became a wall. The students, teachers, and other administrators felt safe because of Tom taking this stand. They also felt appreciated on Valentine's Day when Tom brought them candy.

Although he doesn't get paid a dime for it, Tom stood. He knew this was his fight. Because he stood as a wall, our church was able to stand for one family whose children attended Briarglen. Their mother suddenly died, and because our men were standing as a wall under the leadership of Tom O'Malley, one of our pastors was called to be with the family and walk with them through this tragedy.

Tom O'Malley is a wall. He picked the right fight and he is winning.

"GO" and Pick the Right Fight

Mark Pepin is another example of a guy who knows what it is to pick the right fight. Mark is a young man (for Tom, young was a while ago). But age doesn't matter when it comes to picking the right fight. Mark is an astute businessman with a passion for missions. He loves to do the work of Jesus. He found his fight as he heard me speaking one Sunday morning about Jesus' method of reaching the community. I happen to believe that Jesus wants us to be spiritually passionate and socially relevant. I challenged the people in our congregation to consider becoming part of a ministry that I wanted to launch called GO Teams.

The vision for GO Teams was simple. Groups of people would "go" into the community around our church and find people in need. We would take our spiritual passion into the community, identifying the widow, the orphan, the shut-in, the poor, and the elderly. I knew our community had plenty of these kinds of people because I'd been walking around the neighborhood and praying myself. I had asked God to show us where we could put Him on display. Where could we stand on His behalf? Where could we be a wall?

Mark Pepin stepped up and said he would be the point man for the GO Teams. This meant sacrificing many Saturday mornings to be in the neighborhood, mow lawns, repair broken fences, replace windows, and do whatever else needed to be done.

During one of the GO Team events in the neighborhood, Mark and his wife met some elementary-school-aged girls and started bringing them to church. Because of Mark's selfless commitment, our GO Teams became a known commodity in the community and earned us the right to be heard in the lives of people in the neighborhood.

Mark Pepin is standing as a wall. He picked the right fight, and he is winning.

Picking the Right Fight in the Cave

Quiet guys, loud guys, impulsive guys, patient guys—doesn't matter where you fit in. In the cave you can learn to hear God and then know how to pick the right fight. The friends I've mentioned in this chapter are all in caves practicing the five stones. God is affirming them in their three roles. As this occurs, these men become more and more effective at identifying the right fights. What they've done is become effective at an ancient military tactic.

Major John Buford used the same idea just before the historic battle of Gettysburg during the Civil War. Because of his actions, the North won the ensuing battle. Other military names have become more famous than Buford, but no one's actions were more important to the securing of a victory at Gettysburg than his.

On July 2, 1863, Buford was the unassuming commanding general for the North's First Cavalry Division. On that day, Buford's forces—although greatly outnumbered—quickly and strategically secured the "high ground" on Seminary Ridge. The major's forces secured and held this ground while weathering a two-and-a-half-hour assault by A.P. Hill's Confederate Third Corps. This victory allowed the Union command to sit in a high position and watch the Confederate army's movements. And it enabled Union commanders to know what the Confederates planned to do before they even had a chance to do it. The Confederates would have to march and fight an uphill battle, assuring a Union victory.

Buford picked the right fight. He was strategic. He didn't foolishly engage the Confederates on ground he was sure to lose. Rather, he was wise and strategic and secured the best ground, permitting him to see what the enemy was attempting against his forces.

Use the Five Stones

CaveTime and the utilization of the five stones can help men secure the high ground in their lives. When a man or group of men get some stones and show up for CaveTime, they learn to recognize the movements of the enemy, pick the right fights, and walk in victory. They prepare themselves for success. They receive affirmation in their manhood and walk in their masculine roles. They make better decisions and posture themselves for God to work in their lives.

Allow me to suggest a strategy to help you pick the high ground, to learn to fight the right fights in your life, and to be the masculine presence that God intends for you to be. When you follow this strategy, you get to the high ground—spiritually speaking. Once there, you look down on the enemy and sling some stones at him by doing the following:

Stone 1. Make a decision to *show up* to the cave each day. Pick a time. If space permits, set up a cave where you can escape and get to the high ground. If you aren't a sit-in-a-cave kind of guy, put on your headphones, turn up the worship music, and go for a run, bike ride, or a hike.

Stone 2. Make a decision to vocally and verbally *worship* your God in the cave. Play some worship music and sing along. Turn your face to God and worship Him (maybe even say "OOOOOOORRRRAAAHHHH" a time or two). Read a Cave Psalm out loud (Psalm 18, 34, 52, 54, 56, 57, 59, and 142). The *CaveTime: A Worship Experience* CD is also a great tool. You can purchase it at www.CaveTime.org, or on iTunes.

Stone 3. Make a decision to have conversations in *prayer* with God in your cave. Talk to Him about your concerns, responsibilities, fears, debts, distresses, and discontentments. Here's a suggested weekly outline that allows you to pray for all the people you are responsible for. This is how you start the process of being a wall.

Monday: Have a conversation with God about your closest relationships (these include your wife, kids, nearest friends). Spend time in this conversation each day of the week.

Tuesday: Have a conversation with God about relationships that are one step away from your closest relationships (these are friends and acquaintances, extended family, co-workers).

Wednesday: Have a conversation with God about where you work or go to school. What problems is your company or school facing? What challenges are you facing in these environments? What do you appreciate?

Thursday: Have a conversation with God about your church. Pray for your pastors, missionaries, the vision of your church, and how and where you might serve there.

Friday: Have a conversation with God about your city, state, and nation. Pray for leaders, issues in the news, people in the news, and groups of hurting people you might help.

Saturday: Have a conversation with God about the world. Pray for specific nations that come to your mind, wars, people groups, missionaries, and places where you might even go serve.

Sunday: Have a conversation with God about your personal relationship with Him. Tell God what you love about Him, the things you're thankful for, angry about, and unconfessed sin. Ask Him to prepare you for church.

Stone 4. Make a decision to interact with the *Word*. Memorize it. Maybe choose a portion of one of the Cave Psalms. Also, meditate on the Word. Choose a three-to-five-verse portion of a Cave Psalm and read it, sit for a minute, read it again, sit for a minute, read it again, and then write down thoughts that come to your mind. Finally, spend some time talking to your band of brothers in the cave about what God is teaching you through His Word.

Stone 5. Ask at least one other man to meet with you for CaveTime. Set a day of the week and time to have CaveTime for one hour, and then show up and do it. Use Stones 1 through 4 as a guide for your time. At the end of your first meeting, set a date and time where the men in your cave will go out and serve somewhere (the poor, elderly, Habitat for Humanity, church, local school). Also, plan some healthy fun (the kind that will help you to "live well"); remember that term when choosing a movie, going to a concert, doing outdoor stuff, grabbing a meal or some coffee, jogging together, hunting, fishing, or any other activity you both enjoy.

As I mentioned in the chapters on the stones, you'll find a section titled "Strap on the Toolbelt: Tools for Practicing the Stones," at the end of this book. Be sure to use this easy-to-find section when you have your own CaveTime or a time in the cave with a group of men.

It's important to remember that there are all kinds of men and all kinds of ways to have fun. Your way isn't the only way that's masculine. Don't look down on guys who like things that are different than you like. If you like country music, it might do you some good to go to a jazz concert. Or if you think that classical is the only kind of music that is "really" music, loosen up and listen to a Brad Paisley or Toby Keith song now and then. Because we are all possessors of the X and Y, don't judge the "fun" that other guys enjoy.

Look what's happening to you! You head to the cave on a regular basis. You are learning to use the five stones. You feel comfortable with your roles as a man, and you are gaining the high ground. You sense that you are looking down on your enemy—the enemy who was once kicking your tail at every turn. You're at a place where you are a wall as you stand as an individual man in your home. And you are also part of a wall of men who stand in your community.

We are called for a purpose
We are called to become
A Mighty Wall for Your people
Binding us as one

Be a Wall for your daughters
Be a Wall for your sons
Heaven come down among us
May Your will be done

Be a Wall for your daughters
Be a Wall for your sons
Heaven come down among us
Let Your will be done

"The Wall" by David Gungor and John Arndt
From *CaveTime: The Escape, A Worship Experience*

To those who proposed to build a wall around Sparta, Lycurgus said, "A wall of men, instead of bricks, is best."

Chapter 12

THE WALL: *A MIGHTY WALL?*

I remember where I was as my daughter said, "Dad, I'm kind of scared to go to school tomorrow."

As I heard the apple of my eye express feelings of fear, I stopped in my tracks and responded, "What? Who? Let me at 'em!"

Funny, I didn't even know who 'em was. I didn't know how many. I didn't know if they were unarmed or if they had fully automatic weapons. In fact, it might not have been an issue regarding her physical safety at all. Her fear might have been not feeling ready to take a math test or problems with a friend.

All I know is that if my daughter felt scared, I was going to make it better.

I would have been concerned if my sons had expressed these same feelings. But for the most part, I found that I handled issues and trained my sons differently. And my protective instinct toward them manifests itself differently too. But when a daughter expresses fear, a protective instinct rises up in a father that is indescribable.

I immediately kicked into protective mode. But I realized that I should probably find out what was scaring her. She shared with me that some arrogant and cocky young men at her school were making highly inappropriate physical advances toward her.

Quickly, I formulated a plan. I would run over them with my truck. Of course that was too extreme, so I would kidnap and threaten them. No, that was pretty extreme too—not to mention against the law, as was the truck thing. Maybe I could stalk them and let them know what it felt like to be scared. No, that might get me into trouble, and most people stay away from a church where the pastor is a stalker.

I assured my daughter that this problem would go away the next day, even if I had to take time off work and walk her to class and sit with her every minute of the day, watch her eat lunch, stand outside of the bathroom when she went in, and never let her outside of my sight. If need be, I would take all of those actions.

She looked a bit shocked and afraid as she processed how embarrassing that would be for her, along with the ramifications to her reputation at school. She didn't want to be the girl with the crazy father who followed her everywhere. She said she thought that might be a bit extreme and said everything would probably work out.

In hindsight, I'm sure that having me as her shadow at school would have been embarrassing for her. But that wasn't the issue. The issue for me was that my daughter—one of the people in this world I hold most dear—was being threatened physically, emotionally, and spiritually. And I would have none of it!

I wanted to be a wall for her. This is what men who are dads were created to do, and nothing would stop me from doing what I needed to.

I formulated a more realistic plan to come between my daughter and her fear as well as the physical enemies who had prompted that fear. To be honest with you, I was offended for my daughter, for our family, and for other young women these guys might try to prey on.

After I cooled down a bit, here's the plan I came up with:

1. I called my attorney and had him draw up cease-and-desist orders naming these young men as the perpetrators of activities that were causing my daughter fear. I planned to look these young men in the eyes and deliver the orders personally.

2. I demanded a meeting with these young men and their families; I wanted to confront them and warn them in

case they planned to approach my daughter inappropri-
ately again in the future.

3. I let the school know that if something wasn't done
to ensure that this behavior would never happen to
my daughter or any of my other three children who
attended that school, they would hear from me again
and we would ramp this thing up.

I put my plan into action immediately, and we never had another
problem.

For some reason my daughter—who was then and is now very
beautiful—didn't get asked out much in high school. The students
probably thought that I was slightly insane and had overreacted. But I
really didn't care. My daughter needed to feel safe. Someone needed to
come between her and that threat and be a wall of protection. I would
take the same actions again a million times. Being her wall was my job
as a father, and I couldn't help myself. My daughter's honor, safety, and
emotional peace were at stake.

In the days and weeks and years that have followed, my heart has
been encouraged whenever she told me how safe she felt because of what
I'd done—even if no one asked her out and her friends thought I was a
bit deranged.

The Making of a Wall

The actions that I took for my daughter Hannah were similar to
those taken by David and his men in 1 Samuel 25:15-16:

> These men were very good to us. They did not mistreat us, and
> the whole time we were out in the fields near them, nothing
> was missing. Night and day, they were a wall around us all the
> time we were herding our sheep near them.

The actions of these men after their training in the cave at Adullam made the people of the region feel safe. These people could sleep well at night and do their jobs during the day with no thought of being robbed or threatened.

David and his men stepped into harm's way so the people had nothing to worry about. This is what I mean by being a wall for the people.

Let's review some of the details pertaining to the escape of David and the 400 and identify some of the steps these men took to become a wall—steps that helped them know where to stand and pick the right fight.

When 1 Samuel was written, a divided kingdom and political unrest caused by King Saul chasing David—who had been immensely popular—led to significant instability.

No national police force or large army existed that could help the residents of small towns and outlying regions live safely. People remained somewhat safe by paying off marauding bands of mercenaries and warlords who would offer them protection at a great price. If the people didn't pay up, the bandits would steal whatever they needed.

But in these verses, the people made a point of saying that David and his men did not steal, nor did they cause the residents of that region to fear them in any way. In fact, to gather provisions, David would send representatives to bless the farmers and ask what could be spared.

This is an amazing report, especially because we know that 400 of these men were in distress, in debt, and discontented when they arrived at the cave (see 1 Samuel 22). These guys were prime candidates to take from the weaker farmers and shepherds in order to pay off their debts, to just be mean because of their previous situations in life, or to take care of the needs of a force of 400 men.

David's men didn't respond in these negative ways, however. Why? They had escaped to the cave, gained the high ground, and picked a fight there.

They learned that in a spiritual sense, they could pick the right fight by escaping to the cave. There, they could show up with God and with each other. (I hope you know where I'm going with this by now.) By showing up, they could get some stones and use them to recapture their masculine roles. They didn't take matters into their own hands, stealing to pay their debts and making themselves feel more secure. Instead, they turned their faces toward God, had conversations with Him, received strategic words from Him, and spent time with a band of brothers.

By having CaveTime, David's men picked the right fight and were equipped to process the issues, thoughts, shame, and fear that had come through the assaults leveled at them. They were changed men. They had picked a fight with the giants intimidating them—by escaping, hiding in the cave, and showing up with God and each other.

To these men (and to us today), this doesn't seem like the conventional way to pick a fight with debts, distress, and discontentment. But we're not in a conventional fight.

Like the men in the cave, we face the fight to have our masculinity restored and our roles reinstated by the One who gives us our masculinity in the first place. We become the type of men who make people feel safe all day and all night long. We become walls of God-honed masculinity, looking for enemies in the lives of those we are supposed to protect and cover. OOOOORRAAAAHHHHH!

Standing as a Wall

The following words from David Gungor's song "The Wall" express in a powerful way the charge that God gives every one of us who carry the X and the Y.

> Be a wall for your daughters, be a wall for your sons, heaven come down among us, let your will be done.

God charges us with being a wall for the people we are responsible for. As we do this, we find ourselves in a place to cover them and call down a blessing upon them: "Heaven come down among us, let your will be done."

At the end of the previous chapter, I suggested some ways you might incorporate the five stones into your weekly schedule, with a focus upon Stone 3: Prayer. I suggested some ways to stand for the people around you who God has placed in your life to care for and protect.

Let's look at the same list and explore ways that you can go beyond prayer and also stand as a wall and be a positive influence for these people.

When a man shows up and steps up as the wall he is supposed to be, he helps shield his people from the enemy's assaults and live full and purposeful lives. But how do you know who to be a wall for? How do you know when to step between the enemy and one of these people?

In the CaveTime model of spiritual formation, a caveman has different spheres of influence. These areas where God strategically places you to live your life as a masculine presence and be a wall for His Kingdom. Often, there are several different areas where a man finds that he has been called to be a positive influence and stand as a wall. Here are some common ones:

Your wife. If you're married, you are responsible to cover your wife and to be a wall for her. Earlier, we talked about the idea of "firstness" and the responsibility each man has to take care of and cover his wife first. You need to spend significant time in conversation with God and with your wife so you can understand how to serve, cover, and be a wall for her.

Your family. If you have children, you must spend time in conversation with them and with God in an effort to know how you can cover and be a wall for them.

The next level. You must also spend time in conversation with God about those who are one step away from your wife and children. These people might include your parents, brothers and sisters, other extended family members, and your close friends.

Some great questions to ask yourself about the people in every sphere of influence—in an effort to get insight from heaven concerning how to be a wall for them—might be:

1. Does this person have any fears I can address through prayer and/or through some action on my part?

2. What am I not doing for these people now that would help them feel safer or be safer if I did do for them?

3. Is anything going on in this person's life that makes him or her feel inadequate or insecure, which I might address?

4. Is a person or group of people making the person in my sphere of influence feel scared, insecure, or inadequate? And how can I help deal with the situation?

In addition to the people closest to us, I believe that as men we have several other areas where God calls us to stand as a wall. This might be the place where you work each day or where you go to school. Some great questions to address with God in conversation about this sphere of influence would include:

1. Are there people at work or school I need to be a wall for?

2. Are there issues at work or school where God wants me to take a stand, speak to, or respond to?

3. How can I make God's name known and represent Him well on the job or at school?

In addition to standing as a wall at your workplace or school, God calls you to stand as a wall in your church. Some questions to address with God in conversation about how to stand as a wall for your church would include:

1. How can I stand as a wall for my pastor and other church leaders?

2. What ministry at my church does God want me to commit my time, treasure, and talents to?

3. Is there a widow, orphan, or someone at my church who I can stand for in a practical way?

Next, I believe that God has created us to stand as walls in our neighborhoods, cities, states, nations, and the world. Some questions to address with God in conversation about these areas of influence include:

1. Does God bring to mind someone who I can do something practical for to relieve his or her burden?

2. Does one issue seem to tug at my heart on a regular basis?

3. Is there a group of people I care and think about more than normal? What can I do to serve them in a practical way?

Finally, other people might not fall into one of these neat categories, yet you seem to have them on your mind constantly. It might be that God has placed a burden on your heart for an area or person or group of people and He wants you to stand as a wall for them in practical ways.

To find the answers to the questions above, you must escape and show up to the cave on a regular and daily basis. God has an agenda for every man and assignments about who and where He wants you to be a wall. Only in the cave can you understand which fights to pick with the enemy and gain strategy from interacting with God and His Word.

Heaven come down among us, and may God's will be done in every one of these areas.

Will You Be a Wall?

In his landmark book *Invitation to a Journey*, Robert Mulholland defines Christian spiritual formation as "a process of being conformed to the image of Christ for the sake of others."[30]

Men were created to stand with God—at times by themselves and at times with their brothers—as a masculine presence on behalf of others.

We weren't created for ourselves. We were created for God and for others. Our lives are not our own, and our lives aren't intended for us to spend on ourselves. David and the men in the cave learned this. This is a very simple concept, but very difficult to learn, because men tend to be a selfish bunch.

You really don't have to read far into Scripture to see God's nature: "In the beginning God created the heavens and the earth" (Genesis 1:1). God created the earth as a gift for humanity. He populated it with animals and plants and gave those to mankind as well. He gave man His own breath and touched him and brought him to life. Then, finally, God gave man the gift of a wife; she was a very good gift—in fact, the best thing on the planet.

Do you see a trend here? God gave and gave and gave and gave. He also gave advice to the man and his wife to not eat of the fruit of a particular tree and left them to enjoy each other and to enjoy what He had given them. However, the man didn't act as a wall for his wife. Instead, he sat next to her and watched the enemy of her soul assault her, play with her emotions, and trick her into eating the forbidden fruit. And then he took a bite himself.

The man who was given X and Y chromosomes—created to be a wall and to be *the man*—did not act as a wall. As a result, man lost everything. He lost his soul, his wife lost her soul, and his family was cursed. The assault had begun.

Yet God provided hope. The hope was a wall of promise that would restore humanity and give men a chance to recapture their masculinity. That hope was realized when God once again gave a gift, spoken of by the apostle John in John 3:16:

For God so loved the world that He gave His one and only son, that whoever believes in Him shall not perish, but have everlasting life.

God established a wall for men by giving the gift of Jesus. God redeemed disfigured and marred masculinity by sending Jesus to be a wall. Masculinity would be redeemed as men were redeemed. God gave. God stepped in between the enemy and men through Jesus.

To be like God, we must also give our lives. Dr. Mulholland's definition of Christian spiritual formation has helped me greatly over the last few years. In addition to his earlier definition, he states:

If you want a good litmus test of your spiritual growth, simply examine the nature and quality of your relationships with others. Are you more loving, more compassionate, more patient, more understanding, more caring, more giving, more forgiving than you were a year ago? If you cannot answer these kinds of questions in the affirmative and, especially, if others cannot answer them in the affirmative about you, then you need to examine carefully the nature of your spiritual life and growth.[31]

Ouch, that hurts! I need to keep going to the cave—maybe start having two or three CaveTimes per day!

In order to be like God, whose masculine image I bear, I must be a giver. Fortunately, God created men to be givers. To give my life as a wall, I must give my masculinity for others. This is what being a man truly is and how masculinity is best expressed.

This is what escaping to the cave in the midst of the enemy's daily assaults is all about. To escape, show up to be with Him, turn my face toward Him, converse with Him, receive instruction from Him, connect with a band of brothers for encouragement in my relationship with Him, and then go out and be a wall for my people.

Of course, I cannot be a wall for anyone unless I first allow someone to be a wall for me. He is the Ultimate Caveman! Can you guess who it is?

*You formed the sea, You formed the ground it
  clings to
And You formed me, You know my days would
  come to...pass
And You see me, in all the trials and troubles
And You chose me, and I am nothin'
  without...You*

*You reached down, from on high and took me
You saved me as Your son I will be...Yours.*

"Formed the Sea" by David Gungor and John Arndt
From *CaveTime: The Escape, A Worship Experience*

*I do not fear an army of lions, if they are led by a
lamb. I do fear an army of sheep, if they are led
by a lion.*

—Alexander the Great

Chapter 13

JESUS: *THE ULTIMATE CAVEMAN*

Just a couple of days ago, my wife sat me down and gracefully confronted me on a couple of issues. She gently let me know that some things in my life were, and I quote, "Ugly. Not Christlike. They don't reflect what you preach and what you teach."

She was right. I was hit between the eyes with the absolute truth that I'm a flawed man. So, I took it to the cave. I mulled it over. I had conversations with Dad about it.

I sensed God letting me know that Lori was right. He also let me know that He loves me and that we could deal with this.

I worshipped. He cleaned off my face. I prayed. He gave me a powerful portion of Scripture to interact with. I took how I was feeling to my cave brothers—my fireteam. They let me know that Lori and God were right. We laughed and had prayerful conversations. A couple of guys opened up and told me that they had the same ugliness. In the cave, we dealt with the ugly assault going on in me and them. We had CaveTime.

As you and I have traveled together through David's time in the cave and looked at how each of us can go to the cave, I could almost hear you saying, "But didn't David make some pretty serious mistakes? I'm pretty sure he broke several of the major commandments—repeatedly—even after his cave experience." The answer is yes, he did. David is definitely an example of a flawed caveman. But then again, aren't we all?

Flawed but Passionate

The other day, a rabbi friend of mine referred to David as a "lovable scamp." David was a passionate man—flaws and all. He was passionate as he pursued God, his various enemies, beautiful women, and—a fair amount of the time—his own agenda.

This sounds like a lot of men today as well, doesn't it? I don't want to make David out to be anything he wasn't. Yet for all his flaws, he knew much about intimacy with God—a very personal God whom he loved passionately and who loved him back passionately as well. Their relationship was punctuated with periods of obedience and disobedience, as well as distance and then repentance. Yet God always welcomed back His shamed and repentant shepherd king.

Sounds like the relationship that many of us have had with God.

Because of David's deep and abiding love for the Father, he continued to come to the Lord in the cave, regardless of the consequences. He understood his Father's grace-filled heart. David knew that God would always be willing to have him come close in spite of recurrent problems with sin. While David made as many major mistakes and suffered as many consequences as any individual in Scripture, he knew how to deal with the mistakes, the assaults, and the pains—even those self-inflicted because of disobedience—that came his way on a regular basis.

Let's review again what David learned during his CaveTime. With his band of 400 cave brothers, David learned how to use his stones effectively. He showed up to be with God, worshipped Him passionately, conversed with Him deeply, received a word from Him strategically, and then united with a group of his closest brothers regularly. Like the good shepherd he was, David also went out and tried to be a wall for God's people. Although he wasn't always successful at life, David passionately pursued the God who could repair him, reshape him, and redeem him time and again.

What a picture of grace exists in their relationship!

Ironically, David's most glaring and pronounced period of sin came while his reign as king seemed to be at its apex. Of course, a lot of people know that David's most well-known sin was his adulterous relationship with Bathsheba and the murder of her faithful warrior husband, Uriah the Hittite. Charles Spurgeon, famous preacher and evangelist, said of this period in David's life:

> Had David prayed as much in his palace as he did in his cave, he might never have fallen into the act which brought such misery upon his later days. [32]

I find this to be a powerful statement about the impact of CaveTime—or the lack of time in the cave—in the life of one of God's most powerful and famous servants. This stands as a challenge to every one of us!

As a man, you need CaveTime. I need it too. You need it in times of assault. You also need it at least as much in times of success and glory. During those times, you might be most susceptible to pride and self-reliance, which always leaves you open to stealthy and secretive assaults from the enemy.

You also need to know that, like David, you will have failures, successes, and more mess-ups. But God will always be waiting at the cave. He wants a relationship with you.

I've often wondered if there's an example of a man who has never messed up—someone who has lived the life of a caveman flawlessly and used his stones perfectly.

Jesus Christ: He Is the Rock

You knew where I was going with this. Jesus is the only perfect caveman who has ever lived. Because He completed His journey perfectly, He can be *the* example and *the* empowering force for every caveman.

Remember, Jesus possesses X and Y chromosomes. He is *the man*, and He can inform us, coach us, and lead us in the pursuit of our masculine roles. Because Jesus was every bit a man, He experienced every aspect of masculine life that we face: the lusts, the trials, the tribulations, and the accusations that assault us all.

Jesus used all of the stones we've discussed. He proved that He knew how to use them at the highest levels of effectiveness, as He picked fights with the devil and all of the powers of darkness. Each time, Jesus prevailed.

However, Jesus isn't just about using the stones; *He is the Rock* out of which all stones come! He is the source of the stones. Jesus claimed to be and is the all-encompassing and foundational rock of our faith. He can restore us in our minds, bodies, and spirits. He can teach us about and restore our roles and our masculinity because He came to this planet and operated in them perfectly.

In Matthew 16:13-18, Jesus had a famous conversation with Peter regarding what people said about who He was. In that interaction, He brought up the fact that He was the rock in this way:

> When Jesus came to the region of Caesarea Philippi, he asked his disciples, "Who do people say the Son of Man is?"
>
> They replied, "Some say John the Baptist; others say Elijah; and still others, Jeremiah or one of the prophets."
>
> "But what about you?" he asked. "Who do you say I am?"
>
> Simon Peter answered, "You are the Messiah, the Son of the living God."
>
> Jesus replied, "Blessed are you, Simon son of Jonah, for this was not revealed to you by flesh and blood, but by my Father in heaven. And I tell you that you are Peter, and on this *rock* I will build my church, and the gates of Hades will not overcome it."

When Jesus spoke of building His church upon the "rock," I don't think He was speaking of Peter, as many have asserted. Instead, Jesus was doing two things.

First, Jesus was affirming Peter's proclamation of who He was. Peter spoke the truth when he identified Jesus as the Messiah, Son of the Living God. And Jesus was validating that truth.

Second, Jesus was likely pointing back toward Himself while saying He would build His church upon "this rock." Essentially, He was saying that "The church will be built on *Me*." Once again, He was agreeing with Peter's proclamation that Jesus was the Messiah by claiming that He was the rock.

Others Point to the Rock

The stones exist to be living remembrances and connection points to the Rock. They put us in a place where we might experience the Rock in fresh, new, and life-changing fashion so that He can re-establish us in right relationship with our God. As we use our stones, we're reminded of the Rock's presence in our lives and His ability to take on and defeat all giants: the giants of debt, distress, discontentment, and even death.

Throughout his Psalms, David repeatedly referred to God as his "Rock," "Fortress," and "Stronghold." In one of the Cave Psalms, Psalm 18:2, David used several terms to describe how God was his rock:

> The LORD is my rock, my fortress and my deliverer; my God is my rock, in whom I take refuge, my shield and the horn of my salvation, my stronghold.

The apostle Paul explains to us that Jesus was the Rock that Moses and the Children of Israel drank from in the desert:

> For I do not want you to be ignorant of the fact, brothers and sisters, that our ancestors were all under the cloud and that they all passed through the sea. They were all baptized into Moses in the cloud and in the sea. They all ate the same spiritual food and drank the same spiritual drink; for they drank from the spiritual rock that accompanied them, and that rock was Christ (1 Corinthians 10:1-4).

The apostles Peter and Paul—and then Jesus Himself—again spoke of Jesus' status as the Rock in 1 Peter 2:8, Romans 9:33, and Matthew 21:42. Later in his life, when David was king, he asked in this song:

For who is God, save the LORD? And who is a rock, save our God?... The LORD lives; and blessed be my rock; and exalted be the God of the rock of my salvation (2 Samuel 22:32; 47).

We know that Jesus is the exalted One who saves. So David was referring to Jesus, the Rock, in these verses.

In a final affirmation of His "Rockness," in Psalm 61:1-2, David says:

Truly my soul waits upon God: from him comes my salvation. He only is my rock and my salvation; he is my defense; I shall not be greatly moved.

Jesus is our Rock, example, and guide as we escape to the cave. He shows us how to use our stones to kill the giants who intimidate us and the demonic monarchs and death squads that try to assault our masculinity.

The Rock and the Roles

Because Jesus was tempted, tried, and tested like every other man who has ever walked on the planet, He knows exactly what it feels like to be a man. Jesus was fully man and He lived with the privilege and challenge of walking in the three masculine roles.

Let's review these roles so they are fresh in our minds as we try to understand that what Jesus did relates to every man. The masculine roles are:

Role 1: To have an individual and personal relationship with God first.

Role 2: To be a masculine presence on behalf of God to your world.

Role 3: To pursue relationships that help you to live well.

The writer of Hebrews affirms Jesus' victorious masculine journey:

> For we do not have a high priest who is unable to empathize with our weaknesses, but we have one who has been tempted in every way, just as we are—yet he did not sin (Hebrews 4:5).

The apostle Paul describes the power and long-reaching effects of Jesus' victory as He reclaimed men, their masculinity, and their living out their roles successfully:

> Have the same mindset as Christ Jesus: Who, being in very nature God, did not consider equality with God something to be used to his own advantage; rather, he made himself nothing by taking the very nature of a servant, being made in human likeness. And being found in appearance as a man, he humbled himself by becoming obedient to death— even death on a cross! Therefore God exalted him to the highest place and gave him the name that is above every name, that at the name of Jesus every knee should bow, in heaven and on earth and under the earth (Philippians 2:5-10).

So, Jesus became a man of flesh and bones and wrestled with physical, mental, and spiritual assaults and did not fail—ever! He didn't give in to deception, nor did He succumb to the relentless assaults aimed at him by the powers of darkness. He used the five stones and won an eternal victory for all men.

Because of this, Jesus became the ultimate caveman. That's what Paul meant when he said, "God exalted Him to the highest place and gave Him the name that is above every name." There is none higher than "highest."

Jesus won the victory over any assault against your masculinity and your ability to successfully live out the roles that come with being a man. He is the highest ground. To seek Jesus passionately and submit to Him as Lord means that you attain the highest ground. No self-help method, workout plan, regimen of drugs or supplements, or teachings of some spiritual guide, guru, or teacher can do for you what Jesus can. He is the supreme, most significant, ultimate caveman. Showing up in the cave is all about getting the highest ground through a relationship with Jesus, who will establish or re-establish your right relationship with God.

I want to pause here for a moment and allow for you to make Jesus your highest ground if you haven't ever done so. If you don't take this first step, you'll continue to be assaulted by the enemy and have no defense. No high ground or strategy. Your manhood will be stolen from you. You won't know who you are, and there will be no hope. Eventually, you'll spend eternity separated from God.

It doesn't have to be that way. So why not take care of business right now? Have a conversation with God in your own way and in your own words. Let Him know you realize that you can't endure the assaults by yourself and that you've made many embarrassing mistakes. Tell Him that you want to live your life in fulfillment of your masculine destiny and have a one-on-one relationship with Him, based upon Jesus being your Rock and Savior. Be a caveman by submitting to the Lordship of the Ultimate Caveman.

Through the work of Jesus as our Rock, our manhood, our masculinity, and the masculine roles He created us to live out have been redeemed. He is Lord over our masculinity and the roles that come with being a man.

Let's look at how He picked a fight, used the five stones to endure the assaults against Him, and became a wall against the enemy on behalf of every person.

The Rock and Role 1

The first way Jesus redeemed and informed our masculinity can be seen as He lived out Role 1: having an individual and personal relationship with His Father.

Jesus was all about showing up. Remember, this is foundational to having a CaveTime. Jesus was the supreme and ultimate example of using this stone. The writers of the gospels show us how He loved to get with His Father early, late, and often, in a garden, on a mountain, or on the seashore.

He loved to be alone with the Father—just the two of them. He sought to have conversations with Him whenever and wherever possible. You can do the same thing today.

He also loved to use Stone 2, the stone of prayer or conversation.

> Very early in the morning, while it was still dark, Jesus got up, left the house and went off to a solitary place, where he prayed (Mark 1:35).

> Jesus often withdrew to lonely places and prayed (Luke 5:16).

> Jesus went out to a mountainside to pray, and spent the night praying to God (Luke 6:12).

> He took Peter, John and James with him and went up onto a mountain to pray (Luke 9:28).

> After he had dismissed them, he went up on a mountainside by himself to pray. When evening came, he was there alone (Matthew 14:23).

In this last passage, it seems that Jesus dismissed the people from a meeting and then lost track of time when He was alone with His Father in the mountains.

Because I was raised in the mountains of Colorado, I can understand how Jesus could lose track of time as He hung out with His Father, surrounded by beautiful pines, rocks, wildflowers, and the plethora of colors and hues there in the wilderness. As I grew up, my father and I did this often. We fished and talked and laughed together in the mountains. We talked about life and issues I was facing in almost every area of my life. No subject was off limits—and the relaxed setting where we were just alone together away from the pressures of life made it easier to talk. Some fathers and sons find the same kind of time as they tinker together to restore an old engine, as they collect rare coins, or as they serve their wife/mom and surprise her by thoroughly cleaning the house together.

I'm sure Jesus also sought His Father's advice about every area of life. They spoke about which men He should choose as His disciples. Certainly Jesus wanted to know how He would save individuals from their sins. In the Garden of Gethsemane we get a picture of one of their deep and intimate conversations about the possibility of an easier way for mankind to be redeemed rather than a brutal and agonizing death on a cross.

I don't think their conversations had to do solely with Jesus' wish list either. God is a personal being who has a will and an opinion about every aspect of His children's lives. While Jesus brought requests into their conversations, I think He really just loved to be with His Father. He made time to show up.

Jesus also knows what a busy schedule is like, because He had a very busy one Himself as He traveled, worked, preached, cast out demons, healed people, and fought the powers of darkness at nearly every turn. He needed to be with His Father for direction, guidance, life-giving relationship, and restoration from stress and exhaustion. In spite of the pressing demands of His schedule and the redemptive purpose that was ever with Him, He always made time for conversations with His Dad. It was a time to talk about anything and everything.

You can do the same thing. Ask God's opinion about your schedule, what to have for lunch, or what movie to see. This might sound odd, but I encourage you to try it.

Whenever I feel distant from God, I like to pray a prayer like this. If you are feeling distant from Him, you may want to pray a prayer like this one too:

Dad, would You please help me to overcome the stuff that I allow into my life that prevents me from spending time with You and showing up. I want to be a man of no excuses.

Help me fight the excuse that "I'm too tired to show up."

I realize that I need to spend time with You, so please help me to fight the excuse that "I just don't have the time."

Help me re-prioritize. Help me realize the value and necessity of showing up. Help me realize the value and necessity of having conversations with You. I need Your help to get the highest ground in this battle to make my relationship with You the single most important relationship in my life.

Help me. Deliver me. Focus me. Lead me. Help me get some stones and show up to have a conversation. I want Your Kingdom to come and Your will to be done in every area of my life and my schedule.

In Jesus' name,

Amen

The Rock and Role 2

The second way Jesus redeemed and informed our masculinity can be seen as He lived out Role 2: being a masculine presence in the world on behalf of God.

Jesus established a masculine presence on behalf of His Father on many occasions, but each one played out differently. It would take quite a lot of space to elaborate on this, so let's look at four specific examples.

The soiled dove. The first example where Jesus established Himself as a masculine presence is recounted in John 4:1-42 (I suggest you read this passage for added clarity). In this account, Jesus encounters someone I like to call "a soiled dove" at a local watering hole. This Samaritan woman had been with many men and might have even been trying to hit on Jesus (flirt with, for those of you too old to understand this phrase). In response, Jesus does some rather uncharacteristically nice things for a man who wasn't asking for any favors from her in return.

Jesus asked her for a drink and then engaged her in pleasant conversation about water. He spoke of the type of water that would do more for your soul than the purest of waters or Gatorade could ever do for your body.

In her own words, the woman told the people who lived in her village that He "told me everything that I ever did." Based upon her reputation, He revealed to her that He knew some pretty steamy stuff. If anyone could be subject to judging, the Samaritan woman and the entire town knew that it was her.

But there was no judgment from Jesus, only gentle grace.

In fact, Jesus was so unbothered by her soiled reputation that He gave her a job on His team, telling her to go and share what had happened between them with the residents of her village. In this inter-action He used the stone of interacting with the Word as He reasoned from it in a conversation about worship and the Messiah (who was staring right at her). Note that in Jesus' use of the Word, He doesn't condemn her or beat her over the head with it.

He established a gentle, grace-giving, and Word-of-God-focused masculine presence. As a healthy masculine presence for God in this woman's life, He was assertive but redemptive.

Many men have misunderstood their masculine presence, thinking that to be masculine means to be rough and to bully people and to use people for their own ends—especially women. Jesus understood that to be masculine meant to step up first and be a wall of protection. This woman needed a wall of gentle protection; she got it and was redeemed because of it. Jesus simply had a conversation with her. He did not use her for His own sensual pleasures, but instead He affirmed her.

You can follow this example in a really simple way. If you're married, you might ask your wife about her day and then listen to her. Ask two or three follow-up questions. This—and of course, genuinely listening to her answers—helps her know that you care. Tell her to put her feet up, get her something to drink, and do some housework for her (that stuff some label as "feminine"). You can be every bit a man while doing the dishes or the laundry—being a healthy masculine presence in the life of your wife.

An epic battle. Jesus also established a masculine presence in an account recorded in Matthew 4:1-11, where we see the Holy Spirit leading Him to pick a fight with the devil:

> Then Jesus was led by the Spirit into the wilderness to be tempted by the devil. After fasting forty days and forty nights, he was hungry. The tempter came to him and said, "If you are the Son of God, tell these stones to become bread."
>
> Jesus answered, "It is written: 'Man shall not live on bread alone, but on every word that comes from the mouth of God.'"
>
> Then the devil took him to the holy city and had him stand on the highest point of the temple. "If you are the Son of God," he said, "throw yourself down. For it is written:
>
> "'He will command his angels concerning you, and they will lift you up in their hands, so that you will not strike your foot against a stone.'"
>
> Jesus answered him, "It is also written: 'Do not put the Lord your God to the test.'"
>
> Again, the devil took him to a very high mountain and showed him all the kingdoms of the world and their splendor. "All this I will give you," he said, "if you will bow down and worship me."
>
> Jesus said to him, "Away from me, Satan! For it is written: 'Worship the Lord your God, and serve him only.'"
>
> Then the devil left him, and angels came and attended him.

You might remember me saying how much I love a movie where someone picks a fight with evil, stares it in the face, does battle, and ends up as the last man standing. This interaction between Jesus and Satan is an epic battle. Jesus faces the temptations and assaults of the enemy while physically fatigued and famished. The primary tool He uses to secure victory is Stone 4, the Word of God.

Jesus had established a masculine presence by being gentle with the woman at the well, but He was aggressive with Satan as He hurled the stone of the Word at him three specific times.

The pelting Satan received by the Word resulted in three specific retreats on his part. Jesus took every shot that the enemy had to throw at Him, physically, mentally, and spiritually. Jesus stood up to the enemy on every level, and He will help you to stand too. He was ultimately victorious as He stood on the Word, and you can be as well.

Just as Jesus established this masculine presence in the desert, you can establish a masculine presence through using the Word. Again, this isn't difficult. Start by praying with your wife or kids before they go to bed. Or pray with each family member as they leave for their day and include an appropriate Bible verse in your prayers. You might use this simple blessing:

> May the LORD bless you and keep you; the LORD make His face to shine upon you and be gracious to you; the LORD turn His face toward you and give you peace (Numbers 6:24-26).

When you or your family members are scared or anxious, you might want to pray with them, hug them, and speak these verses over them:

> Do not be anxious about anything, but in everything, by prayer and petition, with thanksgiving, present your requests to God. And the peace of God, which transcends all understanding, will guard your hearts and minds in Christ Jesus (Philippians 4:6-7).

Slinging the Word. A third example when Jesus established a masculine presence would have made another great Western movie script. In fact, I think it did.

One of my favorite Western movies is *Tombstone*. This movie chronicles the events surrounding the famous gunfight at the OK Corral in Tombstone, Arizona. The participants in the gunfight were the famous lawman Wyatt Earp, two of his brothers, and their friend Doc Holliday on one side. On the other side were members of the notorious Clanton Gang.

The two groups of men had been embroiled in a long-standing, hate-filled feud. On one particular day, threats were made, and in a hail of gunfire, the Earps were victorious, killing several members of the Clanton Gang. The sheriff of Tombstone, Johnny Behann, was involved in the Clantons' illegal business dealings and was sympathetic to their cause. As their puppet sheriff, he believed that he had the right to arrest the Earps for gunning down his friends.

The scene in the movie depicting these events shows Behann confronting Wyatt Earp, telling him that his brothers and he were under arrest and they should come with him to the jail. Wyatt Earp's response is absolutely classic when he says: "Behann, I don't think that I will let you arrest us today." Then he, his brother, and Doc Holliday just walk away.

I love this! Talk about masculine presence all over the place.

I don't know if events actually took place this way in Tombstone on October 26, 1861, at 3:00 P.M. But it did about 2,000 years earlier—in Nazareth, right after church. What do I mean? Jesus stood up in church and announced—quoting from Isaiah—that He was the Messiah (see Luke 4:1-31). Jesus essentially picked another fight with the devil.

Then Jesus sat down and began to interact with the Word by quoting verses that offended and convicted most of those who were listening to Him. Jesus was slinging the stone of the Word of God at some pretty serious religious giants that day. He got a pretty serious reaction too. The people rushed Him and took Him to the brow of a cliff. This is where the scene began to look like the OK Corral. The people announced to Jesus that they were going to push Him off the cliff. But without a word, Jesus just walked through their midst.

This is powerful. What a masculine presence Jesus was that day! Whole forces of trained riot police are unable to handle mobs like this one in our day. But Jesus—one man, facing a mob—decided like Wyatt Earp: "I am not going to let you kill Me today."

Jesus would only be killed when *He* was ready to lay His life down of His own volition, saying on the cross, "It is finished. Father, into

Your hands I commit My spirit." He wouldn't allow Himself to be killed until His Father had told Him that it was time.

Once again, Jesus used the stone of the Word to establish His masculine presence, as He made a statement affirming who He was. What a masculine presence Jesus was and is and forever will be!

Is there an issue where the enemy is trying to intimidate you—an area where you need to show up and step up? Where might that be? Maybe in your community there's an issue such as hunger or homelessness that you need to address. Maybe you've been taken to the cliff by the enemy and told that you have no influence, no money—ha ha, you're just a nobody. Don't let Satan do that to you.

Or maybe it's something right in your own home. Perhaps one of your kids is distant and you are at the cliff; the enemy is telling you that you can't talk to your child and it's a lost cause. Don't let Satan do that to you.

Do something today as you toss the stone of the Word at the enemy—take one little action and watch what God might do.

Writing in the dirt. The final example of Jesus establishing His masculine presence is found in John 8:1-11:

> Jesus went to the Mount of Olives.
>
> At dawn he appeared again in the temple courts, where all the people gathered around him, and he sat down to teach them. The teachers of the law and the Pharisees brought in a woman caught in adultery. They made her stand before the group and said to Jesus, "Teacher, this woman was caught in the act of adultery. In the Law Moses commanded us to stone such women. Now what do you say?" They were using this question as a trap, in order to have a basis for accusing him.
>
> But Jesus bent down and started to write on the ground with his finger. When they kept on questioning him, he straightened up and said to them, "Let any one of you who is without sin be the first to throw a stone at her." Again he stooped down and wrote on the ground.

At this, those who heard began to go away one at a time, the older ones first, until only Jesus was left, with the woman still standing there. Jesus straightened up and asked her, "Woman, where are they? Has no one condemned you?"

"No one, sir," she said.

"Then neither do I condemn you," Jesus declared. "Go now and leave your life of sin."

Once again we find Jesus using His masculine presence to stand for someone who was an outcast and in serious trouble. And again, we see Him move gently, yet assertively.

On this occasion, an unnamed woman had been caught in adultery and brought out to the street to be stoned to death in accordance with Jewish law. Jesus operated in His masculine presence and stepped between the woman and her accusers, acting as a wall for her.

Remember that as men, God has called us to stand first, and while doing so, to be prepared to stand between the assaulted ones and the shots the enemy takes at them. Jesus did this, asserting His masculinity by writing words or symbols that seemed to offend all of the accusers—so much so, that they all left. Yet again, He was using the stone of the Word.

We don't know for sure what words or symbols he wrote on the ground. But He communicated quite effectively, didn't He? After His communication offended the accusers, He turned to the woman and communicated gently, asking her rhetorically, "Where are your accusers?" Jesus was a masculine presence for her as He became a wall and gently let her know that no one was left to accuse her—Himself included.

He then challenged her to stop living dangerously, saying in a gracious and affirming tone: "Go and sin no more."

How can you be the same kind of powerful, soft, assertive, and redemptive masculine presence that Jesus was for the adulterous woman on that day? You might be able to help in a battered women's shelter, a pro-life ministry, an outreach to prostitutes, or by joining the effort to stop sex trafficking.

Don't merely condemn the darkness of sin. Light a candle with your masculine presence.

I could go on with more examples of Jesus establishing His masculine presence in a myriad of ways, to many different people. He called Herod an "old fox." He told the Pharisees that they were "a brood of vipers." And Jesus even cursed a fig tree. He was so offended at the people making a mockery of His Father's house that He took matters into His own hands and wrecked the place. Yet He also invited children to sit on His lap. He was gentle with lepers as He touched them. Jesus was soft and affirming on one occasion, and then harsh and brash on another. He was prepared to assert and utilize His masculinity when and where He needed to do so, on behalf of others, but always in conjunction with the Word. As the ultimate Caveman, Jesus used His masculinity to communicate God's love, God's protection, and God's correction.

God help us to do the same.

When you find yourself in a situation where you don't know how to operate in your masculine presence, you might simply pray a prayer like this one to live out your second role:

Jesus, please help me be a man who knows how to walk in my masculinity as You did.

Help me to be secure enough to be gentle and soft when needed. Help me to have the backbone to stand when no one else will, on behalf of those who have no protection.

I know that You have created me to be a man for a reason. I also know that You have created me to be unique for a reason, as well. Help me to be uniquely masculine as I represent You.

Thank You for Your example in the Word and may I always use my masculinity in accordance with it. May Your Word guide me and help me to be a wall of masculinity in my world. Amen.

The Rock and Role 3

The third way Jesus redeemed and informed our masculinity can be seen as He lived out Role 3: pursuing healthy community for the purpose of establishing God's Kingdom.

A band of sisters. Jesus was all about relationships. He passionately pursued relationships with His Father as well as with a community of men and women who were committed to His vision. While He didn't have a wife, He did have women—a band of sisters—who were integral to His ministry (see Luke 8:1-3). Because He established a healthy masculine presence with them, they were drawn to Him and felt secure because He did not objectify them sexually or use them for the pleasure that they might give Him through their bodies.

If you are married, next to your relationship with Jesus, your relationship with your wife is vital to your wholeness as a man. As husbands, we must be committed to treat our wives as Jesus treated women. He treated them with integrity and gentleness and grace. Further, we must be committed to being a wall for them so that the arrows the enemy shoots at them might be blocked and disempowered. The women in our lives should feel safe and valued by us. When you are committed to helping your wife and the other women in your life feel this way, you'll know that you are following Jesus' steps in fulfilling Role 3.

Are you helping the women in your life be safe? Have you asked them what this would look like? Have you asked them if they feel safe? I challenge you to do so and be ready to take some notes when they answer. Make a list and then do something to be a wall to your wife, your daughter, your female friends, and the women you work with.

Being a wall can entail very simple acts, such as sending your wife an email or a text message during the day to let her know that you're thinking of her. Or find out her favorite store and surprise her with a romantic card with a gift certificate inside. Or find out what she is most worried about, pray for it, and ask her about it again later.

In an effort to be a wall for your daughter, spend time with her. You might have to do some girly stuff to be a real man. Play dolls with her, build her a dollhouse, or go to a show or play that you might not usually choose. Put on your best suit and tie and take your daughter on a date.

To be a wall for the women at your workplace or school, be a man of honor. Hold doors, speak honorably, and don't get involved in joking about women in a sexual fashion.

Jesus informed and redeemed our masculinity to the point where He can help us gain the highest ground in our relationships with the women in our lives.

A band of brothers. Jesus also handpicked a group of men that He worked with and through to bring His message of redemption and salvation to the world. He knew that the stone of masculine community was powerful and necessary in the lives of men if they were to be fulfilled in their manhood and walk in their masculine roles.

Once again we see healthy masculine relationships at the core of the emphasis of Jesus' life. These relationships were purposeful and bonded with Jesus as the common denominator. He stood at the center of the disciples' reason for being with each other in the first place.

Sure, it's possible for you to have friends who aren't followers of Jesus, but that group of men will never be as bonded as a band where Jesus is at the center. I believe relationships with a band of brothers can be closer than relationships with blood related family. So did Jesus. In Luke 8 we find an account of Jesus teaching with a huge crowd around Him. His family came late to the meeting and wanted Him to give them special seating or some type of attention. So they sent a message to Him from His mother that they were there and would like for Him to come outside.

To their request He responded: "My mother and brothers are those who hear God's word and put it into practice" (Luke 8:21) Wow! What a statement as to the bond that exists between those of us in the family of God. Jesus is the focal point of God's Word. He is the point of the redemptive story. To follow Him and the example of His life and teachings is to put God's Word into practice.

Men who do this are bonded in the deepest of ways—deeper than by blood.

Jesus informs and redeems our third masculine role in many ways, but I would like to focus upon three of them.

First, Jesus and His band of brothers were bonded by a Kingdom focus. They weren't sports focused, money focused, woman focused, or business focused. These men were focused on furthering the Kingdom of God. Jesus just flat-out called His band of brothers to Kingdom service from day one. In Mark 1:16-20, we read how He called Peter to start fishing for real *big* fish instead of those little ones that he was catching—saying that Peter would catch men for God if he joined Jesus' band of brothers.

Jesus called Levi the tax collector to follow Him (see Luke 5:27-32) and somehow convinced Levi to throw a banquet at his house where Jesus had a chance to minister to sinners.

Each of the disciples was called to a Kingdom vision that challenged him to serve God and tell the redemptive story. These men didn't become part of this band of brothers—whose efforts have resulted in seeing countless numbers of people redeemed—because they just aimlessly hung out together. Their brotherhood was based upon a vision to reach the lost.

I urge you to seek out a band of brothers who have a vision and a heart for the lost. They might be found at your church, but God has led me to some other great friends with whom I could start a CaveTime. Some of them became deep and true friends.

Second, I believe that within the context of being bonded and banded by a Kingdom focus, Jesus and His brothers had fun. We know He liked to go to a good party. In John 2:1-11, we read about Jesus and His band of brothers attending a wedding party where the host ran out of wine. At the request of His mother, Jesus stepped onto the scene and turned water into wine. In fact, the wine was of the highest caliber. Of course it was! I think that it must have been hilarious to have seen the response on the guys' faces who brought the pots filled with water as they served wine out of them just minutes later. How about the host? This is the kind of stuff that I am sure that Jesus and His friends spoke and laughed about around the campfire.

How about the time when Jesus walked out to the disciples across the water and they thought He was a ghost (see Mark 6:45-52)? That's funny! The disciples were in the boat at night, and Jesus walked on water. I'm sure they thought He was a ghost and they were going to die! It's like He snuck up on them and went, "Boo!"

Other situations such as these must have brought a mischievous smirk to Jesus' face. How about multiplying loaves and fishes? A fish with a coin in its mouth? This is great stuff. Jesus was fun and I have no doubt that these men had times of fun as they served their Lord and worked in His Kingdom.

Do you have a band of brothers you can have healthy fun with? Do you even know what healthy fun is? It's fun that glorifies God. It doesn't degrade men or women in any way. Men bound in Jesus can have fun.

I know a group of guys who do a manly movie night. They get barbecue and watch movies that are honorable, but ones that their wives might not want to watch. The last one was the new *True Grit*. They also watched a great film called *The Eagle*. Some bring their teenaged sons with them. At one of the events, they even stopped the movie and discussed some of the scenes. Another group went camping, another went fishing, and another group of men rode motorcycles to a rally. I also know of groups who read a book and then discuss it. I have some friends who go to concerts with me when some of the old Country and Western greats come to town.

Each possessor of the X and Y has his own taste, and odds are that some other guys nearby will like and laugh at the same things.

The third way Jesus and His band of brothers were bonded was through using the stone of worship. Jesus was a worshipper. In Matthew 26:30, we read that after Jesus and His band of brothers had celebrated communion together, they sang a hymn. Most scholars agree that this hymn was Psalm 116.

This Psalm is sung at the Passover supper, and was written by David as a prophetic proclamation. God had given him a vision of the suffering of the Messiah. The words to this Psalm being sung by Jesus and His men at the Last Supper is a powerful thought to entertain. Jesus would also refer to it in His time of passionate prayer in the Garden, shortly after they had sung it at dinner.

The stone of worship being used by a band of brothers and then by Jesus in the Garden is a powerful spiritual force. These men were worshippers, bound together in Jesus. This bond was continually celebrated and deepened as they used the stone of worship together.

OOOOOOORAAAAAAHHHHHH! Do you have a band of brothers you can worship with? I challenge you to engage in using the stone of worship with a group of other men and watch how God deepens your relationship with them. I encourage you to do this in your group cave. Put on a CD and worship together. Remember that the *CaveTime: A Worship Experience* CD is great for this. You can put it on and sing the words to the songs and then let the instrumental version play and sing it again. All it takes is one guy to start singing, and then the other guys will follow.

If you find yourself with no band of brothers, pray this prayer. Come back to it regularly over the next few weeks as you wait to see how your Dad will answer it:

Jesus. You are the Rock! Would You bring some men into my life who believe this as well? Maybe they are already in my life! If they are, would You please show me who they are and allow us to be bonded and banded in You. Allow me to be in a band of brothers.

In advance I ask You to help that band of brothers be a group of men I can have healthy fun with.

Allow that band of brothers to be a group of men I can worship with. Help us to worship without being embarrassed.

I thank You God that even if I don't have these guys in my life just yet, I will commit to being a caveman and use my stones and be the kind of brother that someone else needs.

Lord, I thank You that You are going to bond me with a band of brothers who will be about seeing Your Kingdom come and Your will being done in our lives as You use us together as a unit—as a wall on the earth.

Amen.

Role Reversal

Through His victorious masculine life, Jesus reversed the fate of the roles that men operate in. All men were doomed as a result of the failure of the original man in the Garden of Eden. Adam abdicated all three of his masculine roles, allowing for masculinity in every generation to be assaulted and attacked.

Masculine roles have been confused and skewed ever since.

By virtue of the fact that Jesus possessed X and Y chromosomes, He was *the man*. He came to this planet and proved that He was in fact *the ultimate man*.

Jesus was the Ultimate Caveman. He picked a fight with the one who had deceived Adam and defeated him physically, emotionally, and spiritually. He used the five stones and became the Rock who is forever the highest ground.

As you call on Jesus and use the stones as He did—and as David and his Mighty Men did—you too will be established in your manhood. When the assaults come—and they will—you'll have the Ultimate Caveman as your guide, together escaping and hiding in the cave.

TOOLS FOR PRACTICING THE STONES

Right up front, let me acknowledge that I will be mixing metaphors in what you're about to read. I know that tools don't go with stones (well, at one point in history, I guess the two words were pretty much synonymous—when stones were *used* as tools).

However, the word *tool* is the best word I can think of for the goal of equipping yourself to "do" or practice the five stones covered in Chapters 6 to 10.

If you like to work on your car, you head to the garage and start tinkering next to the toolbox and all of the right tools. The same holds true if you work on something in the house. You can inefficiently go grab one tool at a time, or you can load up and strap on your toolbelt so you have everything you need in one place.

Think of this section of *CaveTime* like your toolbox or toolbelt. Strap it on!

I want to urge you to use these tools so you can practice the stones each day during your CaveTime.

Stone 1: Show Up

As you prepare to engage in the first, foundational, and most important stone, I recommend that you try one or all of the following ideas in an effort to get the CaveTime process rolling in your life.

Tool 1: Decide to show up. This is an elementary idea. But it's powerful when a possessor of X and Y chromosomes makes a decision to do *anything*. So make the decision that showing up in the cave is of vital importance to you and your ability to fulfill your roles as a man. Decide to show up and then follow through.

Tool 2: Set a date, time, and location. Again, this seems simple. But simple can also be smart. Make an immediate move for your calendar, and plug in dates, times, and locations for your CaveTime.

Work this valuable time into your weekly rhythm and fight for it! Make it your first priority and see what happens. I can almost guarantee two things:

1. You'll find that the enemy of your soul will do everything in his power to keep you from showing up. He'll help you justify why you can't be consistent. He'll whisper to you: "It really isn't that important" or "You're just too busy." He'll tell you that because you travel for work, you can't get it done.

   These excuses are sheep dung (trying to stay Davidic here). Men all over the country have CaveTime on airplanes or while they're driving. Some spread the times out through the day as they complete each of the stones at different locations and at different times.

2. You'll have the deepest and most gratifying relationship with God you ever dreamed possible. When you make CaveTime a priority, you'll become the man you were created to be. You'll learn more about your roles and begin to walk in them. You'll walk in your masculine presence on behalf of the Kingdom of God. But you must pick your fight, and to do so you must respond to these questions:

* What day of the week will I meet?
* What time of the day will I meet?
* Where will I meet?

Tool 3: Ask God to help you show up. Don't underestimate God's power to step in and help you show up, especially in light of the enemy's attack I just warned you about. You need reinforcement before you ever start.

You might want to consider this prayer, or something like it:

> *God, I know that I need to show up for CaveTime. In fact, I want very much to do so. I also realize that when I do show up, I'll be attacked in every way possible by the enemy. I will be attacked by busyness, excuse, and fatigue. Please help me to do all that I need to do to successfully defeat these foes and make it to the cave. Help me (us) think through what day of the week, what time of the day, and where works best for us to meet?*
>
> *You know me, and You know my strengths and my weaknesses. Direct me in the ways that work best for me. I need Your help to show up, and I know that when I request Your help, I will receive it.*
>
> *Please send Your Spirit to guide me.*
>
> *In Jesus' name,*
>
> *Amen.*

Tool 4: Get out of bed you sleepyhead! If you plan to show up to your CaveTime in the mornings, you are going to need to make sure that you get out of bed. Here are several ideas to make sure showing up in the morning is a success:

* Set your alarm on the other side of the room so you can't hit the snooze button so easily.

- Have someone call, text, or email you a reminder. While this won't be the long-term solution for getting up, it can help you form a new habit.

- Have a friend come to your house and meet with you for a group CaveTime. This gives you one more reason to get out of bed.

- Go to bed earlier so you can get up earlier.

- Go to bed hungry so your physical hunger helps you get up.

Tool 5: Tell three to five of your closest friends. Enlist the help of others to hold you accountable and to pray for you as you show up. You might want to ask friends to call, text, or email you during the week to ask how your CaveTime went. You might also want to ask these friends to start praying for you to be consistent and faithful in showing up for CaveTime. The support of faithful friends can be a powerful tool in your quest to show up on a regular basis.

Tool 6: Set your show up time and place where you'll have the best chance to make it. Set yourself up for success for showing up. I suggest setting a day of the week, time of day, and location that make it extremely easy to accomplish showing up. If you're not a morning person, then don't set a goal to get up at 4:30 a.m. Instead, show up over your lunch hour or in your car on the way to work. Be realistic and faithful, and that will help you be successful.

Tool 7: Write "show up" on your hand. This probably sounds "middle-schoolish," but it works for some guys. Maybe make your note obvious but not obnoxious by writing "show up" on the inside of your wrist, right under your palm. If that just isn't feasible for you, maybe write "show up" on a Post-it note and place it on your bathroom mirror or the dashboard of your car. The idea is to get the words in front of your face as often as possible in an effort to remember to get to the cave.

Tool 8: Purchase a "show up" glow-in-the-dark bracelet or "show up" stones. At www.CaveTime.org, we offer several bracelets to help men remember and advertise CaveTime. The one designed to help you get going is black with white letters that glow in the dark and say "CaveTime.org" on one side and "Show Up" on the other. We've also designed stones engraved with the words "Show Up" that can be placed in your pocket during the day and on your nightstand at the end of the day as a reminder to have your CaveTime.

Stone 2: Worship

You'll recall that worship is Stone 2 for an important reason: It sets the tone for having a conversation with God. You can use the following worship tools in your own CaveTime, in group CaveTime, or even in a family CaveTime.

Do you remember our conversation about Psalm 34? David had narrowly escaped his embarrassing situation in Gath with spit on his face but none of his dignity left? He escaped to the cave and engaged in worshipful statement and song. I can picture him in the dark, hiding with a couple of guys as he starts to sing Psalm 34 by himself, "I will bless the Lord at all times" (verse 1). Perhaps then he invites the guys hiding with him to join as he says, "Magnify the Lord with me and let us exalt his name together" (verse 3), and together they sing, "I sought the Lord and he answered me and delivered me from all my fears" (verse 4).

What a great model for CaveTime and how to use Stone 2. I'm not saying this is exactly how you need to do it, but I'm suggesting a place to start. Remember, you've already used Stone 1 by showing up, and now it's time to begin interacting with God. Here are some other tools for using Stone 2:

Tool 1: Recite Scripture. In true Davidic form, speaking or singing the Psalms can be a powerful way to use Stone 2. After you show up, just begin to speak one of the Psalms below. After speaking it a few times, maybe you can even sing it, making up your own melody as you go along. This might feel a bit embarrassing at first, but don't worry, God loves to be worshipped in this way.

After a few sessions of doing this by yourself, you might want to try it with the guys in your group cave. You can speak a line and then let the next guy speak one and so on. This is a way for a group to use Stone 2. Have some instrumental music playing in the background.

Here is a great list of Psalms to use with Stone 2. A few are my personal favorites, and some are Cave Psalms (those David wrote in or about his cave experiences).

Remember, you're not speaking or singing these to just make noise; you want to be making a noise to Him. Speak or sing these to God. You are literally turning your face to your Maker.

> I love you, O LORD, my strength. The LORD is my rock and my fortress and my deliverer, my God, my rock, in whom I take refuge, my shield, and the horn of my salvation, my stronghold. I call upon the LORD, who is worthy to be praised, and I am saved from my enemies. The cords of death encompassed me; the torrents of destruction assailed me; the cords of Sheol entangled me; the snares of death confronted me. In my distress I called upon the LORD; to my God I cried for help. From his temple he heard my voice, and my cry to him reached his ears (Psalm 18:1-6).

> The LORD is my shepherd; I shall not want. He makes me lie down in green pastures. He leads me beside still waters. He restores my soul. He leads me in paths of righteousness for his name's sake. Even though I walk through the valley of the shadow of death, I will fear no evil, for you are with me; your rod and your staff, they comfort me. You prepare a table before me in the presence of my enemies; you anoint my head with oil; my cup overflows. Surely goodness and mercy shall follow me all the days of my life, and I shall dwell in the house of the LORD forever (Psalm 23).

The LORD is my light and my salvation; whom shall I fear? The LORD is the stronghold of my life; of whom shall I be afraid? When evildoers assail me to eat up my flesh, my adversaries and foes, it is they who stumble and fall. Though an army encamp against me, my heart shall not fear; though war arise against me, yet I will be confident. One thing have I asked of the LORD, that will I seek after: that I may dwell in the house of the LORD all the days of my life, to gaze upon the beauty of the LORD and to inquire in his temple. For he will hide me in his shelter in the day of trouble; he will conceal me under the cover of his tent; he will lift me high upon a rock. And now my head shall be lifted up above my enemies all around me, and I will offer in his tent sacrifices with shouts of joy; I will sing and make melody to the LORD. Hear, O LORD, when I cry aloud; be gracious to me and answer me! You have said, "Seek my face." My heart says to you, "Your face, LORD, do I seek" (Psalm 27:1-8).

I will bless the LORD at all times; his praise shall continually be in my mouth. My soul makes its boast in the LORD; let the humble hear and be glad. Oh, magnify the LORD with me, and let us exalt his name together! I sought the LORD, and he answered me and delivered me from all my fears. Those who look to him are radiant, and their faces shall never be ashamed. This poor man cried, and the LORD heard him and saved him out of all his troubles. The angel of the LORD encamps around those who fear him, and delivers them. Oh, taste and see that the LORD is good! Blessed is the man who takes refuge in him! Oh, fear the LORD, you his saints, for those who fear him have no lack! The young lions suffer want and hunger; but those who seek the LORD lack no good thing (Psalm 34:1-10).

O God, save me by your name, and vindicate me by your might. O God, hear my prayer; give ear to the words of my mouth. For strangers have risen against me; ruthless men seek my life; they do not set God before themselves. Selah Behold, God is my helper; the LORD is the upholder of my life. He will return the evil to my enemies; in your faithfulness put an end to them. With a freewill offering I will sacrifice to you; I will give thanks to your name, O LORD, for it is good. For he has delivered me from every trouble, and my eye has looked in triumph on my enemies (Psalm 54).

I was glad when they said to me, "Let us go to the house of the LORD!" Our feet have been standing within your gates, O Jerusalem! Jerusalem—built as a city that is bound firmly together, to which the tribes go up, the tribes of the LORD, as was decreed for Israel, to give thanks to the name of the LORD. There thrones for judgment were set, the thrones of the house of David. Pray for the peace of Jerusalem! May they be secure who love you! Peace be within your walls and security within your towers! For my brothers and companions' sake I will say, "Peace be within you!" For the sake of the house of the LORD our God, I will seek your good (Psalm 122).

Tool 2: Read or sing old hymns. I know this might sound boring. But some of the old hymns are literal battle cries and can really fire you up. Many were also written to teach important foundational truths of the Christian faith and make you feel aware of the awesomeness of your Father.

You might start by speaking these songs, drinking in the powerful messages that they contain. Then sing them if you know the melodies. Again, I urge you to speak and sing these to God—turn your face to Him.

Amazing Grace

1. Amazing grace! How sweet the sound
   that saved a wretch like me!
   I once was lost, but now am found;
   was blind, but now I see.

2. 'Twas grace that taught my heart to fear,
    and grace my fears relieved;
    how precious did that grace appear
    the hour I first believed.

3. Through many dangers, toils, and snares,
    I have already come;
    'tis grace hath brought me safe thus far,
    and grace will lead me home.

4. The Lord has promised good to me,
    his word my hope secures;
    he will my shield and portion be,
    as long as life endures.

5. Yea, when this flesh and heart shall fail,
    and mortal life shall cease,
    I shall possess, within the veil,
    a life of joy and peace.

6. When we've been there ten thousand years,
    bright shining as the sun,
    we've no less days to sing God's praise
    than when we first begun.

Text: John Newton; stanza 6, anonymous
Music: 19th century USA melody; harmony by Edwin O. Excell

The Doxology

Praise God from Whom all blessings flow
Praise Him all creatures here below
Praise Him above ye heavenly hosts
Praise Father, Son, and Holy Ghost
Amen

Written by: Connie Ruth Christiansen

A Mighty Fortress Is Our God

1. A mighty fortress is our God,
    a bulwark never failing;
    our helper he amid the flood
    of mortal ills prevailing.
    For still our ancient foe
    doth seek to work us woe;
    his craft and power are great,
    and armed with cruel hate,
    on earth is not his equal.

2. Did we in our own strength confide,
    our striving would be losing,
    were not the right man on our side,
    the man of God's own choosing.
    Dost ask who that may be?
    Christ Jesus, it is he;
    Lord Sabaoth, his name,
    from age to age the same,
    and he must win the battle.

3. And though this world, with devils filled,
    should threaten to undo us,
    we will not fear, for God hath willed
    his truth to triumph through us.
    The Prince of Darkness grim,
    we tremble not for him;
    his rage we can endure,
    for lo, his doom is sure;
    one little word shall fell him.

4.   That word above all earthly powers,
no thanks to them, abideth;
the Spirit and the gifts are ours,
thru him who with us sideth.
Let goods and kindred go,
this mortal life also;
the body they may kill;
God's truth abideth still;
his kingdom is forever.

Text: Martin Luther, Translated by Frederick H. Hedge
Music: Martin Luther; Harmony from The New Hymnal for
American Youth

Stand Up, Stand Up For Jesus

1.   Stand up, stand up for Jesus,
ye soldiers of the cross;
lift high his royal banner,
it must not suffer loss.
From victory unto victory
his army shall he lead,
till every foe is vanquished,
and Christ is Lord indeed.

2.   Stand up, stand up for Jesus,
the trumpet call obey;
forth to the mighty conflict,
in this his glorious day.
Ye that are brave now serve him
against unnumbered foes;
let courage rise with danger,
and strength to strength oppose.

3.   Stand up, stand up for Jesus,
stand in his strength alone;
the arm of flesh will fail you,
ye dare not trust your own.
Put on the gospel armor,
each piece put on with prayer;
where duty calls or danger,
be never wanting there.

4.   Stand up, stand up for Jesus,
the strife will not be long;
this day the noise of battle,
the next the victor's song.
To those who vanquish evil
a crown of life shall be;
they with the King of Glory
shall reign eternally.

Text: George Duffield, Jr., 1818-1888
Music: George J. Webb, 1803-1887

Onward Christian Soldiers

1.   Onward, Christian soldiers, marching as to war,
with the cross of Jesus going on before.
Christ, the royal Master, leads against the foe;
forward into battle see his banners go!
(Refrain)
Onward, Christian soldiers, marching as to war,
with the cross of Jesus going on before.

2.   At the sign of triumph Satan's host doth flee;
on then, Christian soldiers, on to victory!
Hell's foundations quiver at the shout of praise;
brothers, lift your voices, loud your anthems raise.
(Refrain)

3. Like a mighty army moves the church of God;
    brothers, we are treading where the saints have trod.
    We are not divided, all one body we,
    one in hope and doctrine, one in charity.
    (Refrain)

4. Crowns and thrones may perish, kingdoms rise and wane,
    but the church of Jesus constant will remain.
    Gates of hell can never 'gainst that church prevail;
    we have Christ's own promise, and that cannot fail.
    (Refrain)

5. Onward then, ye people, join our happy throng,
    blend with ours your voices in the triumph song.
    Glory, laud, and honor unto Christ the King,
    this through countless ages men and angels sing.

Text: Sabine Baring-Gould, 1834-1924
Music: Arthur S. Sullivan, 1842-1900

Be Thou My Vision

1. Be Thou my vision, O Lord of my heart;
    Naught be all else to me, save that Thou art.
    Thou my best thought, by day or by night,
    Waking or sleeping, Thy presence my light.

2. Be Thou my Wisdom, Thou my true Word;
    I ever with Thee, Thou with me, Lord;
    Thou my great Father, I thy true son;
    Thou in me dwelling, and I with Thee one.

3. Be Thou my battle-shield, sword for my fight,
    Be Thou my dignity, Thou my delight.
    Thou my soul's shelter, Thou my high tower.
    Raise Thou me heavenward, O Power of my power.

4. Riches I heed not, nor man's empty praise,
   Thou mine inheritance, now and always:
   Thou and Thou only, first in my heart,
   High King of heaven, my Treasure Thou art.

5. High King of heaven, my victory won,
   May I reach heaven's joys, O bright heav'ns Son!
   Heart of my own heart, whatever befall,
   Still be my vision, O ruler of all.

Ancient Irish hymn, possibly from the 8th century, translated by Mary E. Byrne

Rock of Ages

1. Rock of Ages, cleft for me,
   let me hide myself in thee;
   let the water and the blood,
   from thy wounded side which flowed,
   be of sin the double cure;
   save from wrath and make me pure.

2. Not the labors of my hands
   can fulfill thy law's commands;
   could my zeal no respite know,
   could my tears forever flow,
   all for sin could not atone;
   thou must save, and thou alone.

3. Nothing in my hand I bring,
   simply to the cross I cling;
   naked, come to thee for dress;
   helpless, look to thee for grace;
   foul, I to the fountain fly;
   wash me, Savior, or I die.

4. While I draw this fleeting breath,
when mine eyes shall close in death,
when I soar to worlds unknown,
see thee on thy judgment throne,
Rock of Ages, cleft for me,
let me hide myself in thee.

Text: Augustus M. Toplady, 1740-1778
Music: Thomas Hastings, 1784-1872

Tool 3: Invest in the CaveTime worship CD. As I mentioned
earlier, we have created a tool that might be helpful to you as you
learn to use Stone 2. The tool is a CD titled, *CaveTime: A Worship
Experience.* This CD contains twelve songs written especially for you
as you have your CaveTime. David Gungor and John Arndt, of the
band called The Brilliance, wrote six songs that express what David
and his men might have felt as they lived through their cave experience. The CD has six songs with vocals, and then the same six songs
as just instrumentals. Use these songs as a help in your Stone 2 time,
embedding the words deeply in your heart. This way, when you play
the instrumental versions of the songs, the words will be part of you.
The CD is available at www.CaveTime.org or iTunes.

I've included the words to two of the songs (and look for other words
on the opening pages of the chapters of this book) so you can start to
speak them as you've done with both the Psalms and old hymns.

Your Love Remains

Through the darkness, through the fire, through my wicked
heart's desires, Your love remains
Though I stumble, though I falter
Through my weakness, You are strong, Your love remains
Oh my, my soul it cries
Oh my, my soul it cries out
Soul it cries out,

Soul it cries, it cries, it cries out
Through my failure, through my heartache, through my
    breaking, in my pain
Your love remains, Your love remains

Words and Music by David Gungor and John Arndt

The Wall

You were there through the fire, You were there through it all
Never leaving or forsaking, You were there through it all
Brought me out of the ashes, brought me out to become
A mighty wall for Your people, may Your love make us one
We are called for a purpose. We are called to become
A mighty wall for Your people, binding us as one
Be a wall for your daughters, be a wall for your sons, heaven
    come down among us
May Your will be done.
Be a wall for your daughters, be a wall for your sons
Heaven come down among us, let Your will be done

Words and Music by David Gungor and John Arndt

Stone 3: Prayer

What does prayer look like in a CaveTime experience? I am going to urge you to jump in with both feet and practice a "Daily Presence" model of prayer. This will help you fulfill Role 2, being a masculine presence for God.

A Daily Presence model means having a daily focus for your prayers, which will help you be able to live out your masculine presence in a more determined and effective manner.

The "Daily Presence" Model

You'll put together a journal where you can record your responses to the prayers that you'll pray each day. God has placed men in the lives of specific people, organizations, geographic locations, schools, churches, and everywhere else that men live in order to be a masculine presence on His behalf. He uses men to see His "Kingdom come and his will being done on earth as it is in heaven."

Your journal pages might look like this—Part 1 is the template, and Part 2 provides information about who/what to pray for each day of the week:

Part 1

Daily Focus Guide for: _____ [day of the week] _____ .

Focus: _____ [person, group, or issue you are praying for] _____ .

Scripture: _____ [write out a verse or brief passage that applies to the person or area you are praying about] _____ .

Words for: _____ [words, thoughts, plans, or verses that come to mind when praying for this person, place, or issue, and ways you can be a wall for them] _____ .

Repeat this process until you are covering a group of people. Five to seven is usually a good number; if you list too many, your prayer time won't have depth.

Part 2

Daily Focus Guide for Monday

Focus: On Monday, focus on the people you are closest to, including your wife and children and perhaps a few very close friends or family members. While you'll pray for the people listed here every day, spend concentrated time praying for them on Mondays.

These questions can help you decide who to list here:

1. Who looks to me for protection, food, shelter, and the basic necessities of life?

2. Who do I feel responsible for?

3. Who are the three to five people I feel the closest to?

Scripture: I use these verses to help me remember that God desires for me to be a wall for my wife and my children:

> Husbands, love your wives, just as Christ loved the church and gave himself up for her to make her holy, cleansing her by the washing with water through the word (Ephesians 5:25-26).

> LORD, what are human beings that you care for them, mere mortals that you think of them? They are like a breath; their days are like a fleeting shadow...Send forth lightning and scatter the enemy;...Reach down your hand from on high; deliver me and rescue me...Then our sons in their youth will be like well-nurtured plants, and our daughters will be like pillars carved to adorn a palace (Psalm 144:3-12, selected verses).

Words for: The following show some ways that I have prayed for my wife, my children, and closest extended family members:

> *Lori: Father, I love You and I ask that You would help me to pray today. Yesterday I was depressed and felt like I was a failure in several different areas of my life. I felt like my prayers were weak. I couldn't concentrate. I thank You that my performance has nothing to do with Your power, nor does it have anything to do with how You are able to cover my people. Thank You for the gift of Lori. I don't understand her all of the time, and I'm sure she doesn't understand me either. Help us to be drawn toward each other, even when we have been distant.*

I ask that You would bring her the perfect peace that comes from her mind being focused on You. Help me to know what's really going on inside her, so that I can help her feel secure and safe and content. I pray that You'll give her the desires of her heart. Please keep her healthy and full of life—full of Your life.

Lord, Your Kingdom come and Your will be done in her, now, today, please. God, please give me something tangible that I can do to be a wall for Lori. In Jesus' name, Amen.

Jacob: *I thank You for Jacob and the fact that he is our first-born. Please protect him from the specific attacks the enemy has aimed at him because he was our first son. Would you confound and scatter any plans that the enemy has for him? May he feel rooted and deep in You, regardless of where he is. He is gifted; please help him see where You want to use those gifts. Please visit him with dreams in the night and words from You during the day. Let words from even strangers confirm what he hears from You in his heart. Your Kingdom come and Your will be done in Jacob. God, please give me something tangible that I can do to be a wall for Jacob. In Jesus' name, Amen.*

Hannah and Mark: *I thank You for Hannah and Mark (her husband). Would You please continue to bless them in their first years of marriage? I ask that the blessings would be relational, financial, and spiritual. May they be relationally open to what is going on in the others' lives. May Hannah be adorned with Your beauty and grace internally and externally as well. May they be financially blessed, so that they can help each of the ministries they have a burden for. As Hannah prepares to teach, I ask You to equip her for that specific group of students that You will have for her. Give her a burden for those kids and their families now. Your Kingdom come and Your will be done in Mark and Hannah. Please give me something that I can do to be a wall for them. In Jesus' name, Amen.*

Caleb: *Thank You for Caleb and for the leadership gift You've placed on him. Let him be wise in where he chooses to use it. Let him lead for the right reasons and in the right direction. What is it that You have for him, Jesus? Please visit him in the night with dreams and visions that are indelibly etched into his mind and his heart. May his visionary nature see visions of what You want and pursue those, not what he wants. Your Kingdom come and Your will be done in Caleb's life. Please give me something to do so that I can be a wall for Caleb. In Jesus' name, Amen.*

Cody: *Thank You for Cody and the many gifts that he has. Help me as his father to tend those gifts well. Help me listen to him. He is so responsible; please don't let me forget that he is there. He is a worshipper, Jesus; help me prod him to put himself out there and worship You often and in front of others, because when he does, people follow him. His new school this year is huge; help him to not just feel like another number, but to know that he is on Your radar screen and You know exactly where he is and what is going on in him. Your Kingdom come and Your will be done in Cody's life. God, please give me something to do for Cody, so that I might be a wall in his life. In Jesus' name, Amen.*

Myself: *I pray that You would deliver me from myself. I tend to be selfish and focused on what's going on in my own world instead of how I can help Your purposes come about in others. I am a sinner. I need Your help. Dad, I need help to put my wife Lori first. I know that in order to love You well, I must love her well, but I only do this half of the time (at best). Please change this about me. Help me to take one practical step to make her feel preferred above me. Please do this in me, God. You have my permission to hammer me and remind me.*

I am bitter today, and I have held a grudge against a couple of brothers. I hate the way that I feel toward them, but I don't know what else to do. You told me in Matthew 5:44 to love people who I don't get along with and those I feel have used me. You know who they are and I pray for them. I don't feel love toward them now, but I know that love is not a feeling; it is a decision. Help me to decide to love them. Would You help the feeling to follow? I desperately want to see Your Kingdom come and Your will be done in me. God, what do You want to do in me? What do You want for me to know? Help me Daddy. In Jesus' name, Amen.

Daily Focus Guide for Tuesday

Focus: On Tuesday, focus on those who are one step away from the people in your Monday group. These would be extended family members, relatives, and good friends.

These questions can help you decide who to list here:

1. Next to the people in your Monday group, who are you closest to?

2. Who looks to you for care, covering, or security and is not in your Monday group?

Scripture: I use these verses to help me remember that God desires for me to be a wall for my extended family and friends:

Fear the LORD, you his holy people, for those who fear him lack nothing. The lions may grow weak and hungry, but those who seek the LORD lack no good thing. Come, my children, listen to me; I will teach you the fear of the LORD. Whoever of you loves life and desires to see many good days, keep your tongue from evil and your lips from telling lies. Turn from evil and do good; seek peace and pursue it (Psalm 34:9-14).

Words for: The following shows a way I have prayed for extended family and close friends:

> *Dad, I ask for You to give me clarity as to how to best relate to relatives I don't regularly see. Please cover them and provide them with all of the good things that they need. As far as my relationships with them, what should I do? Should I call them? Write them? Is there anything that I should pray for in their lives? Would You help me to know what to do in relation to Jerry, as his big deal fell through today and he will not get a commission. Do You want us to help them with groceries? We are barely making it as it is, but what do You want us to do? This economy is crazy, and I am fearful. But I know that You are in control and You are my source. You are Jerry's source too. Please provide for him. I know that You are a loving Dad. Will You do it through me? In Jesus' name, Amen.*

Daily Focus Guide for Wednesday

Focus: On Wednesday, pray for your workplace (or school). Pray for specific people God brings across your path. Ask how He wants you to plant seeds toward their salvation. How can you do some good works for them in an effort to put Jesus on display in practical fashion?

These questions can help you decide who to list here:

1. Who is your boss? Do you feel led to pray for him or her for any reason?

2. What might be some specific ideas to help with the success of your workplace?

3. Are there any people for whom you feel a specific burden to pray for their salvation?

4. Are there any projects or ideas for good works that you might attempt to put Jesus on display?

Scripture: I use these verses to help me remember that God desires for me to be a wall for the people I work with (or go to school with):

> Our barns will be filled with every kind of provision. Our sheep will increase by thousands, by tens of thousands in our fields; our oxen will draw heavy loads. There will be no breaching of walls, no going into captivity, no cry of distress in our streets. Blessed is the people of whom this is true; blessed is the people whose God is the LORD. (Psalm 144:13-15)

Words for: The following shows a way I have prayed for the people I work with (my workplace is the church where I serve as senior pastor):

> *You are the Great Shepherd. Thank You for allowing me to tend Your sheep. I love the leadership team that I work with—they are a dream team. I'm appealing to You to really help us repair our building. I mean Your building. The kitchen and the gymnasium are in broken-down condition, and the youth and children's areas need much help. There are many areas in our church that are in disrepair and need to be renovated. We have a big vision for this part of the city, and we want to be able to serve the great people who live on this side of town. Will You bring us a miracle?*
>
> *We are almost totally volunteer staffed, and we get by on very little. We are growing though! You are bringing new people, and we are reaching out to the neighborhood. We are standing in the school cafeteria and taking care of widows and others who need help. I get depressed at times, wondering if You will bring the miracle. Some days it feels as if the enemy is prowling and not only seeking to devour, but actually doing it. Will You use us to fight him? You are the Mighty God, our Strong Tower, on this side of the city. May Your name be praised in us and through us. Your Kingdom come and Your will be done at our church as it is in heaven.*

Daily Focus Guide for Thursday

Focus: On Thursdays, pray for your neighbors. Walk around your block (or drive if you live in a more rural area) and pray for those you know by name. If you don't know your neighbors by name yet, this is a great chance to do so. As you get to know your neighbors, you'll find out issues occurring in their lives as well as issues in your neighborhood that you can be praying for on a regular basis. Jesus will bring people into your path you can be a wall for—maybe an elderly person, shut-in, or single parent who needs help.

These questions can help you decide who to list here:

1. Who are your neighbors? Do you know their names? Their kids' names?

2. What issues are going on in their lives, and how can you pray for them? Disputes between neighbors? Death in a family?

3. How can you respond directly and in a caring way to any of these issues?

Scripture: I use these verses to help me remember that God desires for me to be a wall for my neighbors:

Sing to the Lord a new song, for he has done marvelous things; his right hand and his holy arm have worked salvation for him. The Lord has made his salvation known and revealed his righteousness to the nations. He has remembered his love and his faithfulness to Israel; all the ends of the earth have seen the salvation of our God. Shout for joy to the Lord, all the earth, burst into jubilant song with music; make music to the Lord with the harp, with the harp and the sound of singing, with trumpets and the blast of the ram's horn—shout for joy before the Lord, the King. Let the sea resound, and everything in it, the world, and all who live in it (Psalm 98:1-3).

Words for: The following is an example of how I have prayed for my neighbors:

Dad, what do You have for me to do in my neighborhood? I pray that You will make Your salvation known to the families who live around our home. This has been a tough neighborhood to integrate into. Are there any issues I can pray for? There seem to be segments of people who stay with their own groups. Is there something that I might do to cross those lines? There are also some neighbors who don't seem to get along. Is there something that I can do about this? Do You want me to be involved? We are the new people here, and it has been tough to fit in. How involved should I get in this neighborhood's issues? There have been some robberies lately, Dad; would You please keep evil away from our homes? Keep the devil from motivating people to break into our homes. I hate robbery, and I suspect that You do too. I might even say that I hate robbers. Is that sin? I want to be Your man on my street. Are there other believers here? Your Kingdom come and Your will be done here where I live. In Jesus' name, Amen.

Daily Focus Guide for Friday

Focus: On Fridays, focus on the city and state where you live. Pray for the mayor and city government officials, governor and state government officials, and national officials that come from your area and represent you in Washington, D.C. In addition, pray for any issues that come to your attention or that you feel a particular burden for. These might be issues such as a drought, poverty, joblessness, sex trafficking, crime, and so forth.

These questions can help you decide who to list here:

1. Who is the city council member (or equivalent) for the area where I live?

2. Who is the mayor in the community where I live?

3. Who represents me at the state level?

4. What locally elected leaders represent me in Washington, D.C.?

5. What issues have I heard about on the news or elsewhere locally that hit me hardest and give me a great burden for the people involved?

Scripture: I use these verses to help me remember that God desires for me to be a wall for my local government officials and issues that I am burdened for locally:

The earth is the LORD's, and everything in it, the world, and all who live in it; for he founded it on the seas and established it on the waters. Who may ascend the mountain of the LORD? Who may stand in his holy place? The one who has clean hands and a pure heart, who does not trust in an idol or swear by a false god. They will receive blessing from the LORD and vindication from God their Savior. Such is the generation of those who seek him, who seek your face, God of Jacob. Lift up your heads, you gates; be lifted up, you ancient doors, that the King of glory may come in (Psalm 24:1-7).

Words for: The following is an example of how I have prayed for my city and state:

Father, I am asking that You speak to our Mayor Bartlett and Governor Fallin. I pray that they would listen to You and if they do not, that You remove them from office. I know that this is a strong prayer, but I desperately want for Your name to be known in our city and our state. Lord, I feel a real pull to be involved with what is going on over in east Tulsa, by the church. There seems to be something going on over there that is causing the economy to falter and poverty to set in.

Please show me and our leadership team what we must do in order for our church to be built up internally and externally as we seek to live out the vision that You have given us to come in and love You and go out and love people. What must we do to renovate our church, so that we might represent You well to that part of the city? We need a miracle in order to renovate the building. I want for it to look like, smell like, and function like heaven. We have a long way to go. You are our Hope. You will help us lift up our heads. You will help our gates to be lifted up and renovated too! Glory to Your name. Give us favor in the eyes of the authorities in this city. Strategic relationships, O God. Show us Your plan. The hearts of the authorities are in Your hand, and Your hand is guiding us. Same hand, same God. Your Kingdom come and Your will be done in our part of the city. In Jesus' name, Amen.

Daily Focus Guide for Saturday

Focus: On Saturday, focus on praying for the United States and other nations God places on your heart. Pray for the President, whether or not you voted for him or her. Pray for the current Vice President and any cabinet members who come to your mind. Pray for the Justices on the Supreme Court bench who have to make key and even life-changing decisions on important issues. In addition, pray for any national issues that you find yourself thinking about or that weigh on you heavily: wars, the economy, moral issues (abortion, same-sex marriage), presidential elections, and so forth. And finally, also pray for any nations that come to mind or that weigh heavily on your heart. This might include people groups that you sense God placing on your mind.

These questions can help you decide who and what to list here:

1. Who are the top elected leaders in my country?

2. Who are the influential appointed leaders at the national level?

3. What wars are taking place I need to be aware of?

4. What sensitive issues that our country struggles with has God placed on my heart?

5. What do I need to pray about concerning my freedom of religion and other freedoms? How can I pray for other nations or people groups who don't enjoy the same freedoms?

Scripture: I use these verses to help me remember that God desires for me to be a wall for my nation and all nations.

> The LORD foils the plans of the nations; he thwarts the purposes of the peoples. But the plans of the LORD stand firm forever, the purposes of his heart through all generations. Blessed is the nation whose God is the LORD, the people he chose for his inheritance. From heaven the LORD looks down and sees all mankind; from his dwelling place he watches all who live on earth—he who forms the hearts of all, who considers everything they do (Psalm 33:10-15).
>
> Sing to the LORD a new song; sing to the LORD, all the earth. Sing to the LORD, praise his name; proclaim his salvation day after day. Declare his glory among the nations, his marvelous deeds among all peoples. For great is the LORD and most worthy of praise; he is to be feared above all gods. For all the gods of the nations are idols, but the LORD made the heavens. Splendor and majesty are before him; strength and glory are in his sanctuary. Ascribe to the LORD, all you families of nations, ascribe to the LORD glory and strength (Psalm 96:1-7).

Words for: The following is an example of how I have prayed for my nation and the Lakota Native American Nation (using Psalms 33:10-15 and 96:1-7 as templates):

> *Lord, I thank You that You foil the plans that the enemy has against our nation, its people and its leaders; You thwart the*

purposes of terrorists and destructive people against us all. But Your plans, Lord, stand firm forever, the purposes of Your heart through all generations. Blessed is the nation whose God is the Lord; may the US and all nations see a revival and call upon You as their Lord. From heaven You, Lord, look down and see all mankind; from Your dwelling place You watch all who live on earth—You who form the hearts of all, who considers everything we do. Please form our hearts to be in line with Your will and Your purposes (Psalm 33:10-15, adapted for a presence prayer for the nations).

Jesus, may the Lakota sing to You a new song; sing to You, all the earth. May the Lakota sing to You, praise the Name; may they proclaim Your salvation day after day. May the Lakota declare Your glory among the nations, Your marvelous deeds among all peoples. For great are You Jesus and most worthy of the praise of the Lakota; may You be feared above all of their gods. For all of their gods are idols, but You made the heavens. Splendor and majesty are before Him, and may the Lakota come bow before Him; strength and glory are in His sanctuary and may they praise His name. Ascribe to the Lord, all you families of the Lakota, ascribe to the Lord glory and strength all you of the Lakota tribe (Psalm 96:1-5). In Jesus' name, Amen.

Daily Focus Guide for Sunday

Focus: On Sunday, pray for the Church. This is a great day to pray for the efforts of your local church, the other churches in your city, and the Church of Jesus Christ at large.

These questions can help you decide who to list here:

1. Who is your pastor? Pastoral staff? Elders?

2. What are the issues that your church is facing? Outreach plans? Budget issues?

3. What does God want for you to do to become totally engaged in the vision of the church?

4. How much of your time, treasure and talent does God want you to give to your church?

Scripture: I use these verses to help me remember that God desires for me to be a wall for His church.

> I rejoiced with those who said to me, "Let us go to the house of the LORD." Our feet are standing in your gates, Jerusalem. Jerusalem is built like a city that is closely compacted together. That is where the tribes go up—the tribes of the LORD—to praise the name of the LORD according to the statute given to Israel. There stand the thrones for judgment, the thrones of the house of David. Pray for the peace of Jerusalem: "May those who love you be secure. May there be peace within your walls and security within your citadels." For the sake of my family and friends, I will say, "Peace be within you." For the sake of the house of the LORD our God, I will seek your prosperity (Psalm 122).

Words for: As I pray for my church each Sunday morning, I pray that the people will come in with their hearts prepared to worship and receive the Word. I also pray that God will help them become totally immersed in the vision of our church as families. I pray that our offerings will be more than enough and that the people will be blessed by giving them. The following is an example of how I have prayed for my church using Psalm 122 as a template:

> *I rejoiced with those who said to me, "Let us go to our church this morning." Our feet are standing in Your gates, the neighborhood by the church is built like a city that is closely compacted together. Jesus, please bring the families, walking and driving down the streets—they are the tribes of the Lord, they will call on Your name—they will praise the name of the Lord, according*

to the vision that You have given to us. Jesus, I am excited that You will be there to save them and to touch them and to give them hope. I pray for the peace of the neighborhood: "May those who love You there be secure. May there be peace in the apartment complexes and security all around." For the sake of the families and friends who live there, I will say, "Peace be within you." For the sake of Your house, Jesus, we will seek to bring the hope and life and prosperity to that place, things that only You can bring (Psalm 122, adapted for a presence prayer). In the name of Jesus I pray, Amen.

Stone 4: Word

To help you interact with God's Word and become proficient at using Stone 4, I want to make a few suggestions:

Tool 1: Get the Word into You

Prepare: Consider singing Psalm 23 as a prayer, asking God to be your shepherd and speak to you through His Word. When you do this, you actually engage in Stone 2, worship, Stone 3, prayer, and Stone 4, interact with His Word.

Again, you might want to get the *CaveTime: A Worship Experience* CD and sing along with the *CaveTime* version of Psalm 23, titled "Shepherd Strong":

Lord, my shepherd strong
I shall not want, You lead me to pastures
To quiet waters,
Restore my soul
And though I walk, through death's own shadow
I fear no evil, thy rod and staff, they comfort me

Lord, my shepherd strong
You lead me on
A table's before me, among my enemies

Anoint my head
Surely Your love and goodness shall follow
All of my days, I will dwell here
All of my days

Choose: Select a short passage of Scripture (two to eight verses), such as a portion of one of the Cave Psalms. These Psalms are as follows: 18, 34, 52, 53, 54, 56, 57, 59 and 142. A passage that has been a huge help to me recently has been Psalm 142:1-6:

> I cry aloud to the LORD; I lift up my voice to the LORD for mercy. I pour out before him my complaint; before him I tell my trouble. When my spirit grows faint within me, it is you who watch over my way. In the path where I walk people have hidden a snare for me. Look and see, there is no one at my right hand; no one is concerned for me. I have no refuge; no one cares for my life. I cry to you, LORD; I say, "You are my refuge, my portion in the land of the living."

Read: Start by asking God to speak to you through the passage you have chosen; read through the words slowly and attentively two or three times; thank God for working in your life through His Word; read the passage slowly and attentively two or three more times.

Interact: After reading the passage for the last time, sit for a few minutes and think about the words you've read. Ask God to touch you and teach you through His Word. Ask Him to make the Word come alive in you.

To help, write down words or phrases that stand out to you or grab your attention. In addition, write down any impressions or thoughts you have. Think about whether or not these impressions might be applied to anything you prayed about in your time of prayer. Take a look back at your Daily Focus Sheets.

Say thanks: Thank God for moving in your life as a result of interacting with this text. Here's a sample prayer of thanks you might want to use as a guide:

Father, thank You for giving me Your Word. It is alive, and it's now alive in me! Please empower it to do its work. I am a willing vessel. Use me. Confront me, if necessary. Please help me change as a result of Your living Word within me. In the areas where I seem to be stuck in my life, will You please teach me? Where there seems to be darkness, will You lead me in the light? Where I am not acting in love, will You please soften my heart? Thank You for Your Word. Thank You for Your life. Thank You for Your plan. And as always, I pray that Your Kingdom would come and Your will would be done in every area of my life as it is in heaven. In the name of Jesus. Amen.

When we have done the training, using the Word of God like an offensive weapon is the easy part. Getting it *into* us and letting it become *part* of us is the groundwork. Allowing it to flow out can be as simple as opening our mouths and speaking what we've been studying.

Using the Word of God to bless, encourage, protect, and strengthen those we know and love is essential, as is rebuking and warring against the enemy of our souls. People are changed by the Word of God, spoken by us, especially when we are sensitive to the Holy Spirit's timing and direction.

Tool 2: Interact with S.O.A.P.

S.O.A.P. stands for Scripture, Observation, Application and Prayer. You can use this method for getting more out of your time in God's Word.

When you enter this part of CaveTime, read the Bible as you normally would. Underline or make note of any verses that jump out at you with special significance. This is the basis for diving deeper and using S.O.A.P.

Scripture: The verse or verses that stuck out to you in your reading; write them down.

Observation: What did you observe about the Scripture that struck you?

Application: How can you apply the observation so that it affects your life today?

Prayer: Pray to God based on what you just learned and ask Him to help you apply this truth in your life.

Tool 3: Sacred Reading

Lectio Divina is an ancient method of interacting with the Word using four "moments."

Moment 1, lectio (reading): In this moment, read the passage slowly and attentively. Write down words in the passage that "stick out" to you or grab your attention.

Moment 2, meditatio (meditation): In this moment, think about the words or phrases that stuck out to you and grabbed your attention.

Moment 3, oratio (prayer): In this moment, ask God to touch you and teach you through this passage. Ask Him to make the Word come alive in you.

Moment 4, contemplatio (contemplation): In this moment, focus on God and think about who He is, as well as what He will do in and through you as a result of interacting with His Word. You might have an idea, plan, or application you want to act on as a result of this time. Write it down and pray about it for several days, seeing what God might be doing.

Stone 5: Community

Finally, some suggestions to help you with Stone 5: the pursuit of community:

Tool 1: Community with Your Wife

I suggest that you start by praying for your wife first, every day of your life. Pray a prayer like the one that I prayed in the tools under Stone 3: Prayer.

In addition, find out what her desires are and write them down. Write them in your Daily Presence Journal under her name and ask God to use you to help make these things come to pass. If you don't know what your wife's desires are, ask her. She might be a bit suspicious at first, but assure her that you aren't angling for something from her. Find out if there are some projects around the house that she has been reminding you about. Or is there a restaurant she has been wanting to go to?

If so, make a reservation and take care of the details yourself (for example, find acceptable babysitting, choose and iron your own clothes, and be on time for your "date"). How about a movie she has been wanting to see?

Finally, speak the Word of God about her. This is what Paul means when he speaks about washing her with the water of the Word. Here is a great verse to start with—just insert your wife's name in the blank when you say the prayer:

> _NAME's_ heart is steadfast, O God, _NAME's_ heart is steadfast. She will sing and make music. Awake _NAME's_ soul! Awake harp and lyre! _NAME_ will awaken the dawn. _NAME_ will praise You, O Lord among the nations; _NAME_ will sing of You among the peoples. For great is Your love, reaching to the heavens; Your faithfulness reaches to the skies. Be exalted, O God, above the heavens; let Your glory be over all the earth (adapted from Psalm 57).

As you spend time in God's Word, write down verses like these and create prayers on your own. You can do it! By doing this, I believe your wife will respond. As you continue using Stone 5, you will undoubtedly have some awesome community with her. You will be living well with your wife.

Tool 2: Community with Other Women

So what if you're not married? How can you pursue healthy relationships with women? I have a few ideas for you as well:

1. Don't treat every interaction with a single woman as if she is *the one*. This is repellent to the ones who are secure. Secure women will think that a man who is too forward and marriage-crazy is either insecure, sex-crazed, or maybe both.

2. Don't objectify women by looking at pictures of them in print or on the Internet for your own pleasure, as this will greatly hamper your relationships with real women.

3. Learn how to be friends with women via worshipping God with them.

4. Participate in healthy co-ed sports leagues, outreach-oriented projects at work or church (such as Habitat for Humanity, a homeless ministry).

5. Serve in a ministry at your church where both men and women serve together.

6. Pray that God would help you to be sensitive as to when *He* wants for you to pursue a deeper relationship with a female, and then ask your CaveTime brothers if they will pray with you and help you discern God's will.

7. Remember that you are a man, possessor of X and Y chromosomes, regardless of whether or not you are in a relationship with a woman. Your masculinity was given to you by your Creator, not a woman.

Tool 3: Community with Other Men

Most men aren't part of a cave. While it's imperative for you to show up and engage in the CaveTime process on your own, in order to operate in Role 3 and live well, you need Stone 5: Community.

So how do you pursue Stone 5 as it relates to your band of brothers—your healthy masculine community? You might already have a group of brothers in your life who help you to live well, but if you don't, the following pointers can help you use Stone 5 effectively in healthy community with other men.

Pointer 1: Start praying in your own* CaveTime *that God will bring you a band of brothers: This is huge! When you're in your own cave, ask God to bring you some brothers so you can be part of a masculine community that helps you live well. Ask Him to make it obvious to you when they come across your path. Start praying for them now.

Pointer 2: Find a church culture that values the type of masculine community that helps you live well: We all know that there are many types of masculine communities available. But not all of them help you live well.

I urge you to head toward a church that will challenge you to be a wall for your people. Look for a place that values relationships and helps you operate in your three masculine roles.

You might look for the following:

1. Are there opportunities for men to serve in the community? Go and serve.

2. Are there opportunities for men to be transparent and speak with other men about what's going on in their lives?

3. Are there Bible studies and activity groups where men engage in healthy activities together?

Get proactive. Go hunting.

Pointer 3: Once you are at a place that values the stones and roles, begin to share your story: As you start to attend church and/or men's events, begin to look for opportunities to share your story. Talk about how CaveTime isn't a typical Bible study. Share that it is a way to learn about how to express your masculinity, as well as hear, worship, and serve God. Talk about the assault that David and his men faced and how you have dealt with the very same attacks. Talk about what has changed you and made you a better husband and father. Your story is a powerful tool.

Maybe set up a time to have a CaveTime with other guys who are interested. Remember to include the pastor in these plans, just to keep him in the loop. He can be a great help in your efforts.

***Pointer 4: Have an introductory one-hour group* CaveTime:** Follow up with the guys who express a desire to have a CaveTime. Maybe call, text, or email them to remind them about the location and time of the meeting. I like to introduce guys to the CaveTime concept by telling my story and how I have been changed. Tell the story of David and how he escaped to the cave and then how the 400 arrived there as well.

Endnotes

Chapter 1

1. James Macnamara, *Media and Male Identity: The Making and Remaking of Men* (New York, NY: Palgrave Macmillan, 2006), quoted in "Men Become the Main Target in the New Gender Wars," University of Western Sydney (November 27, 2006): http://www.physorg.com/news83863660.html, accessed on 9/23/2009.

2. Meg Meeker, *Boys Should Be Boys* (Washington DC: Regnery, 2008), p. 9.

Chapter 2

3. F.B. Meyer, *David: Shepherd, Psalmist, King* (Fort Washington, PA: CLC Publications, 2007), location #913-921.

4. Eugene Peterson, *The Pastor* (New York, NY: HarperOne, 2011), p. 106.

5. Cliff Graham, *Day of War: Lion of War series* (Grand Rapids, MI.: Zondervan, 2011), p. 144.

6. http://dictionary.reference.com/browse/distress, accessed on 1/10/2012.

7. *The New John Gill Exposition of the Entire Bible*, http://www.studylight.org/com/geb/view.cgi?book=1sa&chapter=022&verse=002, accessed on 1/10/12.

8. Graham, p. 9.

9. "Consumer Debt Statistics," http://www.money-zine.com/Financial-Planning/Debt-Consolidation/Consumer-Debt-Statistics/, 1/1/2012, accessed on 1/17/2012.

10. "Stress Over Debt Taking Toll on Health," http://www.usatoday.com/news/health/2008-06-09-debt-stress_N.htm, 6/9/2008, accessed on 1/16/2012.

11. "The Return of Debtors Prisons: Thousands of Americans Jailed for Not Paying Their Bills," http://thinkprogress.org/justice/2011/12/13/388303/the-return-of-debtors-prisons-thousands-of-americans-jailed-for-not-paying-their-bills/, 12/13/2011, accessed on 1/16/2012.

12. *John Gill's Exposition on the Whole Bible*, http://www.biblestudytools.com/commentaries/gills-exposition-of-the-bible/1-samuel-22-2.html, accessed on 1/16/2012.

13. "Students Borrow More Than Ever for College," *The Wall Street Journal* online-9/4/2009, http://online.wsj.com/article/SB10001424052970204731804574388682129316614.html, accessed on 1/19/2012.

14. "What happens with Student Loan Debt if you Leave the Country?" eHow Money, 5/26/2011, http://www.ehow.com/info_7752856_happens-debt-move-another-country.html, accessed on 1/19/2012.

15. "Student Credit and Debt Statistics," http://www.credit.com/press/statistics/student-credit-and-debt-statistics.html, 12/31/11, accessed on 1/19/2012.

16. *Hebrew-Greek: Key Word Study Bible*, Key word #s 5253/5883, *Spiros/Kodhiates* (Chattanooga, TN: AMG, 1996), pp. 1971, 1980.

Chapter 3

17. In C.S. Lewis's *The Lion, the Witch and the Wardrobe*, the four children who enter Narnia are taken by the Beavers to see Aslan, the King. However, when they discover that he is a lion, they become concerned and ask whether or not he is safe. The answer is, "Who said anything about safe? 'Course he isn't safe, but he's good. He's the king, I tell you." This is the sentiment I am expressing in my story as I beheld the Rockies. They were created by a God who is good but not safe, just as the mountains are good but not safe.

18. "Injury in Colorado," Colorado Department of Public Health and Environment, www.cdphe.state.co.us/pp/injepi/InjuryinColorado/11other unintentional.pdf, 2007, p. 119, accessed on 1/23/12.

19. See Tremper Longman III & David E. Garland, General Editors, *The Expositor's Bible Commentary* (Grand Rapids, MI: Zondervan, 2008), pp. 202-203.

Chapter 4

20. F.B. Meyer, *David: Shepherd, Psalmist, King* (Fort Washington, PA: CLC Publications, 2007), locations 792-800; Cliff Graham, *Day of War* (Grand Rapids, MI: Zondervan, 2011), locations 42-48.
21. Richard G. Rogers, "Marriage, Sex, and Mortality," *Journal of Marriage and the Family* 57 (1995), pp. 515-516.

Chapter 5

22. Cliff Graham, *Day of War* (Grand Rapids, MI: Zondervan, 2011), locations 1458-1464.

Chapter 7

23. "The Dark Night of the Soul," by Saint John of the Cross, translation by A.Z. Foreman, (http://poemsintranslation.blogspot.com/2009/09/saint-john-of-cross-dark-night-of-soul.html, accessed on 2/4/2012.
24. Albert Barnes, *Notes Critical and Explanatory Practical on the Book of the Prophet Isaiah* (London: Knight and Son, 1852), p. 281.
25. "Turn Your Eyes Upon Jesus," words and music by Helen H. Lemmel, 1922.

Chapter 8

26. Dallas Willard, *The Spirit of the Disciplines* (San Francisco, CA: Harper, 1999), p. 184.

27. Graham, location 1936. In *Day of War,* author Cliff Graham records a fictitious conversation between two of David's men, where they speak about David using the term *Ab*, instead of Yahweh. Some commentators believe that David may have used the term *Ab*, which meant Father, for God. This was more intimate than the other formal names that were used for Him, many of them unspoken. In a personal conversation, Semitic language expert, Dr. Donald Vance, Professor of Biblical Languages at Oral Roberts University, verified that David might have used this term for God; if he did, it could have meant that he was attempting to be more informal with Him.

Chapter 9

28. Tim Hansel, *When I Relax I Feel Guilty* (Elgin, IL: Chariot Family, 1979), pp. 51-52.

Chapter 10

29. *John Gill's Exposition of the Bible,* http://www.biblestudytools.com/commentaries/gills-exposition-of-the-bible/2-samuel-1-26.html, accessed on 2/13/2012.

Chapter 12

30. Robert Mulholland, *Invitation to a Journey* (Downers Grove, IL: InterVarsity, 1993), p. 15.

31. Ibid., p. 42.

Chapter 13

32. Charles Spurgeon, *Treasury of David* (Grand Rapids, MI: Kregel Publications, 1976), p. 654.

ABOUT JEFF VOTH

Dr. Jeff Voth has a doctorate in leadership and spiritual formation, a master's in philosophy and apologetics, and a master's
in divinity. He is a seminary professor, lead pastor at a church that
focuses on community outreach, and the founder and president of
CaveTime.org. Jeff reveals that most of his life's advanced learning
has come from time in his cave, just as David's did—a place of
refuge and safety, and a place to hear God's voice and gain courage
for the battle. Jeff is marred to Lori, his wife of over twenty-five
years, and they have four children.

CAVETIME.ORG

Are you ready to come to the cave? Bring all that you are, and all that you are not, and join other warriors who will be a wall for you. At CaveTime.org you can sign up for Jeff's blog, Facebook page, watch special videos, and receive encouragement from other cavemen. It is a virtual cave. All of our Bible studies, books, Cave-Time Manuals, and other materials are available at our virtual cave, CaveTime.org.